Warman's

M.I. Hummel®

FIELD GUIDE
2nd Edition

OFFICIAL
M.I. HUMMEL®
GUIDE

Heidi Ann von Recklinghausen

Published by

Krause Publications, a division of F+W Media, Inc.
700 East State Street • Iola, WI 54990-0001
715-445-2214 • 888-457-2873
www.krausebooks.com

To order books or other products call toll-free 1-800-258-0929
or visit us online at www.krausebooks.com

ISBN-13: 978-1-4402-2997-8
ISBN-10: 1-4402-2997-X

Designed by Sandi Carpenter
Edited by Mary Sieber

Printed in China

Contents

Introduction

Hum 27: Joyous News

The 100-year anniversary celebration of Sister Maria Innocentia Hummel's birth—May 21, 1909—brought forth new interest in Sister Hummel's life, her drawings, her paintings, and the beloved M.I. Hummel figurines, which this book is about. Who would have thought that these cherished figurines, which were introduced by Franz W. Goebel at the Leipzig Trade Fair in March of 1935, would bring such incredible interest around the world shortly after World War II that it continues today?

This book is a reference for the collector, dealer, anyone owning just a few figurines, inheriting a collection, or contemplating starting a collection. New information has been found about existing figurines, rare figurines, as well as the new figurines developed from Sister Maria Innocentia Hummel's two-dimensional drawings, and the 2000 Series, which were sculpted by German master sculptors and produced in Germany.

This is a collector's guide—and nothing more. It should be used in conjunction with every other piece of information you may be able to obtain from other sources such as websites, books, and any seminars you may attend.

For more in-depth information on M.I. Hummel collectibles, see *The Official M.I. Hummel® Price Guide* by Heidi Ann von Recklinghausen (F+W Media, Inc., 2010).

Chapter 1

The Story of M.I. Hummel® Figurines

The story of the Hummel figurines is unique. It is practically required reading for those with an interest in the artist, her work, and the resulting three-dimensional fine earthenware renditions—the famous Hummel figurines.

These charming but simple figurines of boys and girls easily capture hearts. In them we see, perhaps, our son or daughter, sister or brother, or even ourselves when we were racing along the paths of happy childhood. You will love them all with their little round faces and big questioning eyes. These figurines will collect you, and if you have the collecting tendency, you will undoubtedly want to collect them.

You may ask yourself who is the artist who inspired these beguiling figurines. Who is the person with the talent to portray beauty and innocence with such simplicity? The answer is

Hum 7: Merry Wanderer

Berta Hummel, a Franciscan Sister called Maria Innocentia.

Berta Hummel was born on May 21, 1909, in Massing in lower Bavaria, which was located about 40 miles northeast of Munich, Germany. She grew up in a family of two brothers and three sisters in a home where music and art were part of everyday life. In this environment, her talent for art was encouraged and nourished by her parents.

Berta attended primary school between 1915 and 1921. During these early years, she demonstrated the great imagination so necessary for an artist. She created delightful little cards and printed verses for family celebrations, birthdays, anniversaries, and Christmas. Her subjects were almost always the simple objects with which she was familiar: flowers, birds, animals, and her friends. In her simple child's world, she saw only the beautiful things around her.

When she finished primary school, Berta was enrolled in the Girls Finishing School in Simbach in 1921, in order to nurture and train her talent further and to give her a wider scope of education and experience. Here again, her artistic talent was recognized and upon finishing, it was decided that she should go to a place where she could further cultivate that talent and realize her desire to pursue art as a vocation. In 1927, Berta moved to Munich, where she entered the Academy of Fine and Applied Arts. There she lived the life of an artist, made friends, and painted to her heart's content. At the academy, she acquired full mastery of art history, theory, and technique. It was here also that she met two Franciscan sisters who, like herself, attended the academy.

There is an old adage that art and religion go together. Berta Hummel's life was no exception. She became friends with the two sisters and began to think that this might be the best way to serve. Over time, she decided to join the sisters in their pilgrimage for God, in spite of the fact that she had been offered a position at the academy.

For a time, Berta divided her days between her talent for art and her love for humanity and hours of devotion and worship. Then she took the first step into a new life of sacrifice and love. After completing her term as a novice, the 25-year-old took the first vows in the Convent of Siessen on Aug. 30, 1934.

Although Berta Hummel (now called Sister Maria Innocentia) gave her life over to an idea she thought greater than any worldly aspiration, the world became the recipient of her wonderful works. Within the walls and the beautiful surroundings of the centuries-old convent, she created the paintings and drawings that were to make her famous. Within these sacred confines, her artistic desires enjoyed unbounded impetus.

Little did her superiors dream that this modest blue-eyed artist who had joined their community would someday win worldwide renown. Much less did they realize what financial assistance Maria Innocentia's beloved convent would derive from her work as an artist.

During World War II, in 1945, after the French had occupied the region, the noble-minded artist's state of health was broken. On Nov. 6, 1946, at age 37, despite the best care, Sister Maria Innocentia died, leaving all her fellow sisters in deep mourning.

The M.I. Hummel figurines, modeled according to Sister Maria Innocentia's work, are known all over the world. They are her messengers, bringing pleasure to many people.

M.J.Hümmel®

Facsimile of the well-known M.I. Hummel signature.

W. Goebel Porzellanfabrik

In an area near Coburg in northern Bavaria, Franz Detleff Goebel and his son, William Goebel, founded the company in 1871. Once known as Oeslau, the village is now known as Rödental.

Initially, the company manufactured slates, pencils, and marbles, and after 1879, it was well into the production of porcelain dinnerware and beer steins.

By the mid-1910s, a third generation, Max Louis Goebel, had taken the helm of the company and it began manufacturing fine earthenware products. His son, Franz Goebel, became active in the company, and the two of them developed a line of porcelain figurines that was well accepted on the international market.

Upon Max Louis' death in 1929, Franz took over the running of the company along with his brother-in-law Dr. Eugen Stocke, a trained economist, who was the financial manager of the operation.

By the early 1930s, Goebel had gained considerable experience and expertise in fashioning products of porcelain and fine earthenware.

Sister Maria Innocentia's art came to the attention of Franz in December 1933 in the form of religious note cards for the Christmas and New Year seasons. These cards were brand new publications of her art by Ars Sacra Josef Müller Verlag. (This company has since evolved into ArsEdition, well known to collectors of prints and postcards of Hummel art.)

Remarkably, it was in March of the same year that the Siessen Convent had made an unsolicited inquiry of the Josef Müller firm regarding the possibility of reproducing their Sister Maria Innocentia's art.

Once Franz Goebel saw the cards in Munich,

he conceived the idea of translating them into three-dimensional figurines. He sought and gained permission from the convent and Sister Maria Innocentia Hummel. The letter granting Goebel permission stated plainly that all proposed designs must be pre-approved before the product could be manufactured. This is true to this day: The convent still has the final say as to whether a proposed design stays within the high standards insisted upon by M.I. Hummel.

After Franz Goebel gained permission for the company to produce the figurines, it took about a year to model the first examples, make the first molds, experiment with media, and make the first models of fine earthenware. The company presented the first figurines at the Leipzig Fair in 1935. They were a great success, and by the end of 1935, there were 46 models in the new line of Hummel figurines.

Production of Hummel figurines dwindled during the years of World War II, and toward the end of the war, production ceased completely. During the American Occupation, the United

States Military Occupation Government allowed Goebel to resume operation. This included the production of Hummel figurines. During this period, the figurines became quite popular among U.S. servicemen in the occupation forces, and upon their return to the United States, many brought them home as gifts. This activity engendered a new popularity for Hummel figurines. Goebel Porzellanmanufaktur and its master sculptors and master painters continued to produce existing Hummels as well as new Hummels until Sept. 30, 2008, when the company closed its factory in Rödental due to financial strain. Goebel continues producing accessories in the gift and home area.

Manufaktur Rödental GmbH

In February 2009, Manufaktur Rödental GmbH, under the direction of investor and managing director Jörg Köster, began manufacturing Hummel figurines at the original location in Rödental. Original M.I. Hummel team employees were recruited to start the production of Hummel figurines.

Manufaktur Rödental produces the figurines with the same quality and workmanship as before, while maintaining the relationship with Convent Siessen and the Hummel family. "Time for Hummel" is the theme for Manufaktur Rödental, crafting new figurines with new vision and enthusiasm.

Trademark 9 was created to mark the new era of Hummel figurines. (See "Understanding Trademarks" section.)

M.I. Hummel Club

The M.I. Hummel Club worldwide continues its service to current and new members alike. The club celebrated the 100th anniversary on May 19, 2009, of Sister Maria Innocentia's birth on May 19, 1909. A chapter was written for each *Insights* club magazine to commemorate her life. A seminar was given by Joan Ostroff, club ambassador, at the North American 2009

M.I. Hummel Convention held in Buffalo, New York. Ostroff commemorated Sister Maria Innocentia's life by drawing those who attended right into the life of Sister Maria Innocentia. Together with the sisters of Convent Siessen; Jörg Köster, Manufaktur Rödental; Hummel artists; the M.I. Hummell Club; and the convention attendees, a new chapter of M.I. Hummel figurines began.

You can enroll at www.mihummelclub.com or call membership services at 1-800-666-CLUB (2582). The address is: M.I. Hummel Club, M.I. Hummel Company, LLC, 3705 Quakerbridge Rd., STE 105, Mercerville, NJ 08619-9919. If you are interested in joining a local chapter of the club, contact membership services, which will be able to put you in contact with the nearest local chapter in your area.

Chapter 2

Buying & Selling

The single most important factor in any collecting discipline is knowledge. Before you spend your hard-earned funds to start or expand a collection, it is incumbent upon you to arm yourself with knowledge. If you've bought this book, you have made a good start. Now you must study it, learn from it, and refer to it often when you're on your hunt. But don't stop there.

In today's market, there are many sources, some quite productive and some not so productive, as is true of any collectibles field. Supply and demand is a very important factor in the world of Hummel collecting. We have been through some extraordinary times. Nearly four decades ago, retailers had a very difficult time obtaining Hummel figurines and plates in any quantity, never had a choice of pieces, and often went for weeks with none in stock. They often had to order an assortment, and there were three monetary levels of assortments. In addition, it was often two to three months between ordering them and taking delivery. This was true for almost every Hummel retailer in the country. In those years of limited supply, even small dealers would see their shipments gone in a matter of days. There was a time in the late 1970s and early 1980s that dealers not only couldn't meet collectors' demands, but kept lists of collectors and what each collector was looking for. The result was most of their stock was pre-sold, and what was left would sometimes literally be fought over.

The shows and conventions that featured Hummel saw great crowds in those early years of the surge in Hummel popularity. Frequently, the dealers would literally be cleaned out before half the show was over, leaving booths empty of all but tables and display fixtures.

Our economic times have changed all that, but the good news is that the collector still has sources for Hummel collectibles. This is particularly true if you are not specializing in the older trademark pieces. These can be found in

Hum 49: To Market

gift shops, jewelry stores, galleries, and shops specializing in collectibles. Even the popular television shopping programs feature Hummel figurine sales from time to time. They are also available by mail order from various dealers around the country, many of whom also deal in the old trademark pieces.

A great way to find them is by looking in the various antique and collectible publications. Many of them have a classified ad section where dealers and collectors alike offer Hummel figurines and related pieces such as plates.

Productive sources, if you can get to them, are the large annual gatherings of dealers and collectors held around the country. Especially if you're trying to find the older-marked pieces, these shows can be a goldmine. But even if you're a collector of the new pieces, attending the shows is fun and a good learning experience. They usually offer lectures and seminars by experts and dealers, all of whom are subject to much "brain-picking" by crowds of collectors. You also have the opportunity to meet other collectors and learn from them.

The Internet has provided collectors of all sorts of Hummel-related pieces with a place not only to shop, but also to interact in chat rooms or online discussion panels with other collectors. Online appraisal services with trained appraisers can give you a value of your collection for a fee.

Using the Internet, the possibilities for expanding or selling a collection are endless. Take, for example, the number of Hummel-related collectibles on auction websites. The one caution about using the Internet for buying, however, is to beware of potential fraud. Without the opportunity to actually pick up and inspect a piece, it is sometimes difficult to legitimize authenticity. See "E-Buying Tips" for a bit more detail on Internet buying.

You can sometimes find old trademark pieces in shops that sell both new and old pieces. There are a few around the country. With the increased awareness of the value of the older-marked pieces, it is very unlikely—but still possible—that some smaller, uninformed shops could have a few pieces bearing older trademarks, bought some years ago for sale at whatever the current retail price is for the newer ones.

Bargains? Yes, there are bargains to be found. Estate auctions and sales and country auctions are your best bet. Flea markets (especially in Europe), junk shops, attics, basements, relatives, friends, acquaintances, and neighbors are by far the best sources for bargains. In short, anywhere one might find curious old gifts, castaways, etc.

E-Buying Tips

People flock to online Internet sites to shop for a wide array of collectibles. As more opportunities develop for making the best deal, collectors need to educate themselves on the proper methods of buying online, and by doing so, reduce the risk of possible abuse by an unscrupulous merchant.

- Understand how the auction works.
- Check out the seller. For company information, contact the state or local consumer protection agency and Better Business Bureau.

- Beware of out of focus pictures.
- Know when to buy—early morning or "night owl" shopping on an auction site may be beneficial.
- Be especially careful if the seller is a private individual.
- Get the seller's name, street address, and telephone number to check him/her out or follow up if there is a problem.
- Ask about returns, warranties, and service.
- Be wary of claims about collectibles.
- Use common sense and ask yourself: Is this the best way to buy this item? What is the most I am willing to bid?
- Get free insurance through the auction sites whenever possible.
- For assistance, check out these websites: www.fraud.com, www.ftc.gov and www.bbbon-line.com.
- Protect your financial information by using Pay-Pal.

The Price to Pay

The province of this book is primarily Hummel figurines. The preponderance of these collectibles was made by W. Goebel Porzellanfabrik (hereinafter called Goebel).

There are several factors that influence the actual selling price of the old and the new. The suggested retail price list addresses those pieces bearing the current production trademark. Each time the list is released, it reflects changes in the retail price. These changes (usually increases) are due primarily to the basic principle of supply and demand, economic influences of the world money market, ever-increasing material and production costs, the American market demand, and last, but certainly not least, an expanding interest in Germany and the rest of the European market.

The list does not necessarily reflect the actual price you may have to pay. Highly popular pieces in limited supply can go higher and some of the less popular pieces can go for less. This has been the case more in the recent past than now, but the phenomenon still occurs.

The value of Hummel figurines, plates, and other collectibles bearing trademarks other than the one currently being used in production is influenced by some of the same factors discussed earlier, to a greater or lesser extent. The law of supply and demand comes into even more prominent light with regard to pieces bearing the older trademarks, for they are no longer being made and the number on the market is finite. More simply, there are more collectors desiring them than there are available pieces. Generally speaking, the older the trademark, the more valuable or desirable the piece. One must realize, however, that this is not a hard and fast rule. In many instances there are larger numbers available of pieces bearing an older mark than there are of pieces bearing later trademarks. If the latter is a more desirable figure and is in much shorter supply, it is perfectly reasonable for it to be more valuable.

Another factor must be considered. The initial find of the rare international figurines saw values shoot up as high as $20,000 each. At first, the figurines were thought to exist in just eight designs and in only one or two prototypes of each. Over the years, several more designs and multiples of the figurines have surfaced. Although they are still quite rare, most bring less than half of the original inflated value. So you see, values can fall as the result of an increase in supply of a rare or uncommon piece. This situation can be brought about artificially as well. If someone secretly buys up and hoards a large quantity of a popular piece for a period of time, the short supply will drive the value up. If that supply is suddenly dumped on the market, demand goes down. This has happened more than once in the past, but not so much today.

Yet another circumstance that may influence a fall in pricing is the reissue of a piece previously thought by collectors to be permanently out of production. This has happened because of collectors' past confusion over company terminology with regard to whether a piece was permanently or temporarily withdrawn from production. Many collectors wish to possess a particular item simply because they like it and have

Hum 96: Little Shopper

no interest in an older trademark version. These collectors will buy the newer piece simply because they can purchase it for less, although recent years have seen the last of the older trademarked pieces go for about the same. It follows naturally that demand for an even older trademark version will lessen under those circumstances.

You may find it surprising that many of the values in the old trademark listing are less than the values reflected in the current M.I. Hummel suggested retail price list. You have to realize that serious collectors of old mark Hummel collectibles have very little interest in the price of or the collecting of those pieces currently being produced, except where the list has an influence on the pricing structure of the secondary market. As we have seen, demand softens for some of the later old trademark pieces. That is not to say that those and the current production pieces are not valuable—quite the contrary. They will be collectible on the secondary market eventually. Time must pass. Make no bones about it, with the changing of trademarks and the passing of time will come the logical step into the secondary market. The principal market for the last two trademarks is found in the general public, not the seasoned collector. The heaviest trading in the collector market in the past couple of years has been in the Crown and Full Bee trademark pieces. The Stylized Bee and Three Line trademark pieces are currently remaining stable and the Last Bee trademark pieces are experiencing a stagnant market.

Selling M.I. Hummel® Items

There is an old saying in the antique and collectibles world that goes like this: "You buy at retail and sell at wholesale." Although this is true in some cases, it is most assuredly (and thankfully) not the rule. The axiom can be true if you must sell and the only ready buyer is a dealer whose percent discount equals or exceeds the amount your item has appreciated in value. This can also be true if you have consigned your piece to an auction, although auctions usually allow you to set a reserve. A reserve is the lowest price you will sell at. If bidding doesn't reach your reserve, you still owe the auctioneer his fee, but you get your item back. This is the case whether you are dealing with a traditional auctioneer or an online auction site.

There are several other methods of selling, each of which has its own set of advantages and disadvantages. Bottom line—educate yourself about the piece(s) you are selling. This will help know what you have and its approximate worth.

Selling to a Dealer

The have-to-sell scenario is an obvious disadvantage, but selling to a dealer will, in most cases, be a painless experience. If you have been fortunate in your acquisitions and the collection has appreciated considerably, it may also be a profitable encounter. If you are not near the dealer and have to ship, then you run the risk of damage or loss.

Running Newspaper Ads

Selling to another collector in your local area is probably one of the easiest and most profitable ways to dispose of your piece(s). There is the advantage of personal examination and no shipping risks.

Running Collector Publication Ads

This is another fine way to get the best price, as long as the sale is to another collector. The same shipping risks exist here also, and you do have to consider the cost of the ad.

Answering Wanted Ads in Collector Publications

The only risk beyond the usual shipping risks is the possibility of the buyer being disappointed and wishing to return the pieces for a refund.

Selling Through a Local Dealer

If you are fortunate enough to have a dealer near you, he/she may take consignments for a percentage.

Selling on the Internet

Although shipping risks and those related to dissatisfied buyers also apply to Internet sales, one advantage over traditional advertisements is not having to pay to publicize your piece (if you have your own website). Websites also offer an opportunity to showcase not only the basic description of a piece, but also a photograph of it.

If you are not so technologically advanced that you can run your own website, selling via auction sites is relatively inexpensive as well. Such sites also offer a wide range of services, most notably for billing, which helps the seller lessen his/her risks of a fraudulent sale (buyers using bad checks, stolen credit cards, etc.).

Another advantage to selling on the Internet involves the web's far-reaching capabilities. The Internet provides worldwide exposure.

Utilize Collector Club Services

The M.I. Hummel Club has an online "members forum" in the members-only section of the website. A member can ask a question of other members, look for a particular Hummel, or sell a Hummel. There is also a collector's market form on the website that you may use. There is no charge for this service beyond membership dues. You must be a member, so you can enroll at www.mihummelclub.com or call membership services at 1-800-666-CLUB (2582). The address is: M.I. Hummel Club, M.I. Hummel Company, LLC, 3705 Quakerbridge Rd., STE 105, Mercerville, NJ 08619-9919. If you interested in joining a local chapter of the club, contact membership services, which will be able to put you in contact with the nearest local chapter in you area.

Chapter 3
Understanding Trademarks

Since 1935, there have been several changes in the trademarks on M.I. Hummel items. In later years of production, each new trademark design merely replaced the old one, but in the earlier years, frequently the new design trademark would be placed on a figurine that already bore the older style trademark. In some cases, a change from an incised trademark to a surface stamped version of the same mark would result in both appearing on the figure. The former represents a transition period from older to newer, and the latter resulted in what are called "Double Crown." This section is meant to give you an illustrated guide to the major trademarks and their evolution to the trademark presently used on M.I. Hummel items.

Many subtle differences will not be covered because they serve no significant purpose in identifying the era in which an item was produced. There are, however, a few that do help to date

Hum 47: Goose Girl

a piece. These will be discussed and illustrated. The dates of the early trademark changes are approximate in some cases, but probably accurate to within five years or so. Please bear in mind that the dates, although mostly derived from company records, are not necessarily as definite as they appear. There are documented examples where pieces vary from the stated years, both earlier and later. A number of words and phrases associated with various trademarks can, in some cases, help to date a piece.

Note: It is imperative that you understand that the various trademarks illustrated and discussed here were used by Goebel on all of its products, not just Hummel items, until about mid-1991, when a new mark was developed exclusively for use on M.I. Hummel items.

The Crown Mark (TMK-1): 1934-1950

The Crown Mark (TMK-1 or CM), sometimes referred to as the "Crown-WG," was used by Goebel on all of its products in 1935, when M.I. Hummel figurines were first made commercially available. Subtle variations have been noted, but the illustration here is all you need to identify the trademark. Those subtle differences are of no important significance to the collector. The letters WG below the crown in the mark are the initials of William Goebel, one of the founders of the company. The crown signifies his loyalty to the imperial family of Germany at the time of the mark's design, around 1900. The mark is sometimes found in an incised circle.

Another Crown-type mark is sometimes confusing to collectors; some refer to it as the "Narrow Crown" and others the "Wide Ducal Crown." This mark was introduced by Goebel in 1937 and used on many of its products. Goebel called it the Wide Ducal Crown mark, so we shall adopt this name as well to alleviate confusion. To date, most dealers and collectors have thought this mark was never found on a M.I. Hummel piece. Goebel, however, in its newsletter *Insights* (Vol. 14, No. 3, pg. 8), stated that the mark was used "...rarely on figurines," so we assume there might be some out there somewhere.

Often, as stated earlier, the Crown Mark will appear twice on the same piece, more often one mark incised and the other stamped. This is, as we know, the "Double Crown."

When World War II ended and the United States Occupation Forces allowed Goebel to begin exporting, the pieces were marked as having been made in the occupied zone. The various forms and phrases to be found in this regard are illustrated here.

These marks were applied to the bases of the figurines, along with the other markings, from 1946 through 1948. They were sometimes applied under the glaze and often over the glaze. The latter were easily lost over the years through wear and cleaning if the owner was not careful. Between 1948 and 1949, the U.S. Zone mark requirement was dropped, and the word "Germany" took its place. With the partitioning of Germany into East and West, "W. Germany," "West Germany," or "Western Germany" began to appear most of the time instead.

Until the early 1950s the company occasionally used a WG or a WG to the right of the incised M.I. Hummel signature. When found, the signature is usually placed on the edge of, or the vertical edge of, the base. Some have been known to confuse this with the Crown Mark (TMK-1) when in fact it is not.

| Incised
Crown Mark | Stamped
Crown Mark | Wide Ducal
Crown Mark |

The Hummel signature as a base rim marking.

The Full Bee Mark (TMK-2): 1940-1959

In 1950, Goebel made a major change in its trademark. The company incorporated a bee in a V. It is thought that the bumblebee part of the mark was derived from a childhood nickname of Sister Maria Innocentia Hummel, meaning bumblebee. The bee flies within a V, which is the first letter of the German word for distributing company, Verkaufsgesellschaft. The mark was to honor M.I. Hummel, who died in 1946.

There are actually 12 variations of the Bee marks to be found on Goebel-produced M.I. Hummel items, but some are grouped together, as the differences between them are not considered particularly significant. They will be detailed as a matter of interest.

The Full Bee mark, also referred to as TMK-2 or abbreviated FB, is the first of the Bee marks to appear. The mark evolved over nearly 20 years until the company began to modernize it. It is sometimes found in an incised circle. The history of the transition and illustrations of each major change follows. Each of them is still considered to be the Full Bee (TMK-2).

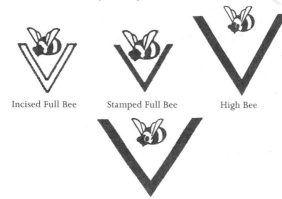

Incised Full Bee   Stamped Full Bee   High Bee

Small Bee. Note that the bee's wingtips are level with the top of the V.

Baby Bee   Vee Bee

The very large bee flying in the V remained until around 1956, when the bee was reduced in size and lowered into the V. It can be found incised, stamped in black, or stamped in blue, in that order, through its evolution.

The Stylized Bee (TMK-3): 1958-1972

A major change in the way the bee is rendered in the trademark made its appearance in 1960. The Stylized Bee (TMK-3), sometimes abbreviated as Sty-Bee when written, as the major component of the trademark appeared in three basic forms through 1972. The first two are both classified as the Stylized Bee (TMK-3), but the third is considered a fourth step in the evolution, the Three Line Mark (TMK-4). It might interest you to know that Goebel reused the Crown-WG backstamp from 1969 until 1972. It is not always there, but when it shows, it is a small blue decal application. This was done to protect

Goebel's copyright of the mark. It otherwise would have run out.

The Large Stylized Bee: This trademark was used primarily from 1960 through 1963. Notice in the illustration that the "W. Germany" is placed to the right of the bottom of the V. The color of the mark will be black or blue. It is sometimes found inside an incised circle. When you find the Large Stylized Bee mark, you will normally find a stamped "West" or "Western Germany" in black elsewhere on the base, but not always.

Large Stylized Bee

The Small Stylized Bee: This mark is also considered to be TMK-3. It was used concurrently with the Large Stylized Bee from about 1960 and continued in this use until about 1972. Note in the illustration that the "W. Germany" appears centered beneath the V and bee. The mark is usually rendered in blue and is often accompanied by a stamped black "West" or "Western Germany." Collectors and dealers sometimes refer to the mark as the One Line Mark.

W. Germany

Small Stylized Bee

The Three Line Mark (TMK-4): 1964–1972

This trademark is sometimes abbreviated 3-line or 3LM in print. The trademark used the same stylized V and bee as the others, but also included three lines of wording beside it, as you can see. This major change appeared in blue color.

Three Line Mark

The Last Bee Mark (TMK-5): 1972-1979

Actually developed and occasionally used as early as 1970, this major change was known by some collectors as the Last Bee Mark because the next change in the trademark no longer incorporated any form of the V and the bee. However, with the reinstatement of a bee in TMK-8 with the turn of the century, TMK-5 is not technically the "Last Bee" any longer. The mark was used until about mid-1979, when Goebel began to phase it out, completing the transition to the new trademark in 1980. There are three minor variations in the mark shown in the illustration. Generally, the mark was placed under the glaze from 1972 through 1976 and is found placed over the glaze from 1976 through 1979.

Last Bee Mark

The Missing Bee Mark (TMK 6): 1979-1991

The transition to this trademark began in 1979 and was complete by mid-1980. As you can see, Goebel removed the V and bee from the mark altogether. Many dealers and collectors lamented the passing of the traditional stylized V and bee, and for a while, called the mark the Missing Bee. In conjunction with this change, the company instituted the practice of adding to the traditional artist's mark the date the artist finished painting the piece. Because the white overglaze pieces are not usually painted, it would be reasonable to assume that the date is omitted on them.

Missing Bee Mark

The Hummel Mark (TMK-7): 1991-1999

In 1991, Goebel made a move of historical importance. The company changed the trademark once again. This time, the change was not only symbolic of the reunification of the two Germanys by removal of the "West" from the mark, but very significant in another way. Until then, Goebel used the same trademark on virtually all of its products. The mark illustrated here was for exclusive use on Goebel products made from the paintings and drawings of M.I. Hummel.

Hummel Mark

The Millennium Bee (TMK-8): 2000-2008

Goebel decided to celebrate the beginning of a new century with a revival in a bee-adorned trademark. Seeking once again to honor the memory of Sister Maria Innocentia Hummel, a bumblebee, this time flying solo without the V, was reinstated into the mark in 2000 and ended in 2008. Goebel stopped production of the M.I. Hummel figurines on Sept. 30, 2008.

Millennium Bee Mark

The Manufaktur Rödental Mark (TKM-9): 2009-Present

Manufaktur Rödental purchased the rights to produce M.I. Hummel figurines from Goebel in 2009. This trademark signified a new era for

Hummel figurines while maintaining the same quality and workmanship from the master sculptors and master painters at the Rödental factory. This trademark has a full bee using yellow and black for the bumblebee, which circles around the words "Original M.I. Hummel Germany" with the copyright sign next to M.I. Hummel. "Manufaktur Rödental" is underneath the circle with a copyright sign.

Manufaktur Rödental Mark

Other Base Marks

There are marks in addition to the U.S. Zone marks already covered that can be found on the bases and backs of Goebel Hummel items.

First of all, there are several colors of marks that you may encounter. The colors found to date are black, purple, red, brown, green, and blue.

The color blue has been used exclusively since 1972. There also have been several combinations of colors found.

The following list contains various words and marks found associated with the trademarks. There are probably more to be discovered, but these are representative.

W. Germany – by W. Goebel (in script)
W. Germany – W. Goebel (in script)
GERMANY - Copr. W. Goebel
Germany - by W. Goebel, Oeslau 1957
WEST GERMANY - *II Gbl. 1948
West Germany - OCCUPIED GERMANY
WESTERN GERMANY - Western Germany

First Issue, Final Issue, and 125th Anniversary Backstamps

Starting in 1990, Goebel began stamping any newly issued piece with the words "First Issue," during the first year of production only. In 1991, the company began doing the same thing during the last year before retiring a piece, by marking each with the words "Final Issue." The words are also accompanied by the appropriate year date. The stamps are illustrated for you here. The first piece to bear the Final Issue backstamp was Hum 203, Signs of Spring, in both sizes.

Goebel's 125th anniversary was in 1996, and all figures produced in that year bear the special backstamp.

W. Goebel mark in script · 125th Anniversary backstamp

Final Issue and First Issue stamps

Mold Numbers and Size Designators

Mold Numbers

All Goebel-made Hummel items were made by the use of molds, and each unique mold was assigned a number. The number is part of the mold and it, along with the size designator, becomes a part of the finished piece. It is generally incised on the underside of the base, but for practical reasons may appear elsewhere on the item.

Until the mid-1980s, it was thought by most collectors that the highest mold number normally used in production was in the mid-400s. Time and extensive research revealed, among other things, that the number in the Goebel design pool most likely exceeds 1,000 by a great deal. A large number of these have not yet been put into production, and those planned are designated Possible Future Editions (PFE) by Goebel. A few of these (presumably in sample form) have somehow found their way into the collector market, but the occurrence is exceedingly rare. When a PFE becomes a production piece, the earlier PFE example almost always bears an earlier trademark than the mark found on the production piece. It, therefore, retains its unique status. Of the remaining designs, some may be PFEs and some may never make it into the collection.

Size Designators

While the mold number was treated as separate from the size designator system, in reality, the two comprise what is sometimes called the Hummel number (Hum number), but more commonly, the mold number.

The system has changed little over the years, but has been modified once or twice.

Beginning with the first commercial piece in 1935 and continuing to about 1952, the first size of a particular piece produced was considered by the factory to be the "standard" size. If plans were to produce a smaller or larger version, the factory would place a "0" (zero) or a decimal point after the model or mold number. Frequently, but not always, the "0" would be separated from the mold number by placing a slash mark (/) between them. There are many cases where the "0" or the decimal point did not appear. Apparently, this signified that at the time, there were no plans to produce other sizes of the same piece. Not all the figures produced before 1952 were designated with the "/0" or decimal point, but if present, it is a great help in beginning to date a figure.

The factory used Roman numerals or Arabic numbers in conjunction with the mold numbers to indicate larger or smaller sizes than the standard.

Roman numerals are normally used to denote sizes larger than the standard, and Arabic numbers indicate sizes smaller than the standard. When utilized in the normal manner, the Arabic number is always found to the left of the "0" designator. A general exception is the occasional use of an Arabic number in the same manner as the Roman numeral. The Roman numeral size indicator is never used with the "0" designator

Mold Numbers and Size Designators

present, and the Arabic number is never normally used without the "0" designator.

We can usually assume that a figure with the mold number and no accompanying Arabic or Roman numerals is the standard size for that model. If the mold number is accompanied by Roman numerals, the figure is a larger size, ascending to larger sizes the higher the numeral.

There seems to be no set standard size or set increase in size for each of the Arabic or Roman numeral size designators used in the collection. The designators are individually specific to each model and bear no relation to the designators on other models.

Common Abbreviations

CE: Closed edition (no longer produced)
CN: Closed number
CE: M.I. Hummel Club exclusive
EE: Exclusive edition for M.I. Hummel Club members
LE: Limited edition
PFE: Possible future edition
TW: Temporarily withdrawn

WARMAN'S M.I. HUMMEL® FIELD GUIDE **55**

Chapter 4

The Original 46

The first M.I. Hummel figurines were presented at the Leipzig Fair in 1935. By the end of 1935, there were 46 models in the new line. Those original 46 Hummels are presented here. They are arranged by Hummel mold number in ascending order, 1 through 46.

You will find the price listings almost complete, but it is impossible to conscientiously assign a value to each and every model that exists today. When it was impossible to obtain pricing information on a particular figure size or variation, the appropriate space is left blank or the listing is omitted altogether. In the latter case, it was not possible to ascertain and document all existing models. From time to time it is possible to establish the existence of a piece but without sure information as to size or trademark. In these cases, the corresponding space is left blank.

The sizes are approximate but as accurate as possible. The sizes listed are those most frequently encountered in those listings and notated as the "Basic Size." Most of the time, this is the smallest size for each figure. Frequently, however, there would be one smaller size listed, but the preponderance of other listings would indicate a 1/4" or 1/2" larger size. In these cases, the larger size was assumed the more representative.

For purposes of simplification, the various trademarks have been abbreviated in the list. Should you encounter any trouble interpreting the abbreviations, refer to the list on the next page.

Hum 11: Merry Wanderer

Trademark	Abbreviations	Dates
Crown	TMK-1	1934-1950
Full Bee	TMK-2	1940-1959
Stylized Bee	TMK-3	1958-1972
Three Line Mark	TMK-4	1964-1972
Last Bee	TMK-5	1972-1979
Missing Bee	TMK-6	1979-1991
Hummel Mark	TMK-7	1991-1999
Millennium Bee/Goebel Bee	TMK-8	2000-2008
Manufaktur Rödental Mark	TMK-9	2009-present

Hum 1: Puppy Love

Puppy Love was first known as the Little Violinist. It was first modeled by master sculptor Arthur Moeller and can be found in Crown Mark (TMK-1) through TMK-6. It was retired in 1988, never to be produced again.

Version 1: The most significant variation occurs in TMK-1. In this variation, the head is tilted to the right instead of the typical left, he wears a black hat, and there is no necktie.

Version 2: This is found in TMK-2 and TMK-3. The boy's head has very little tilt toward his left shoulder.

Version 3: This is the current standard production model. The boy's head is tilted to his left shoulder and is, or close to, touching the violin. This version is found in all trademarks.

Hum No.	Basic Size	Trademark	Current Value	
1	5"	TMK-1	$2,400	Version 1
1	5"	TMK-1	$350	Version 3
1	5"	TMK-2	$400	Version 2
1	5"	TMK-2	$275	Version 3
1	5"	TMK-3	$225	Version 2
1	5"	TMK-3	$245	Version 3
1	5"	TMK-4	$275	
1	5"	TMK-5	$175	
1	5"	TMK-6	$125	

Hum 1: Puppy Love

Hum 2: Little Fiddler

Originally known as the Violinist and then The Wandering Fiddler, this little fellow is almost always wearing a brown derby with an orange hatband. The figure has been made in five sizes since its initial introduction. The two largest sizes were temporarily withdrawn from production in 1989. The smallest, Hum 2/4/0, was introduced into the line in 1984 and was temporarily withdrawn from the North American market on Dec. 31, 1997.

Hum No.	Basic Size	Trademark	Current Value
2/4/0	3-1/2"	TMK-6	$125
2/4/0	3-1/2"	TMK-7 TW	$110
2/0	6"	TMK-1	$550
2/0	6"	TMK-2	$400
2/0	6"	TMK-3	$325
2/0	6"	TMK-4	$325
2/0	6"	TMK-5	$175
2/0	6"	TMK-6	$175
2/0	6"	TMK-7	$175
2/0	6"	TMK-8	$260
2/I	7-1/2"	TMK-1	$550
2/I	7-1/2"	TMK-2	$500
2/I	7-1/2"	TMK-3	$400
2/I	7-1/2"	TMK-4	$450
2/I	7-1/2"	TMK-5	$300
2/I	7-1/2"	TMK-6	$1,200
LE 50 with gold-painted base			
2/I	7-1/2"	TMK-6	$300
2/I	7-1/2"	TMK-7 TW	$200
White Expressions of Youth			
2/I	7-1/2"	TMK-7 TW	$300

Hum 2: Little Fiddler

Hum No.	Basic Size	Trademark	Current Value
LE 200 for guild of specialist china and glass			
2/I	7-1/2"	TMK-7 TW	$300
2/II	11"	TMK-1	$1,300
2/II	11"	TMK-2	$925
2/II	11"	TMK-3	$850
2/II	11"	TMK-4	$825
2/II	11"	TMK-5	$725
2/II	11"	TMK-6 TW	$700
2/III	12-1/4"	TMK-1	$2,000
2/III	12-1/4"	TMK-2	$1,850
2/III	12-1/4"	TMK-3	$1,600
2/III	12-1/4"	TMK-4	$1,400
2/III	12-1/4"	TMK-5	$1,100
2/III	12-1/4"	TMK-6	$1,100
2/III	12-1/4"	TMK-8	$1,550 retail

Hum 3: Book Worm

This figure of a girl reading a book appears more than once in the collection and was originally called Little Book Worm. It is also found in a smaller size as Hum 8 and in the Hum 14/A and 14/B bookends, titled Book Worms, with a companion figure of a boy reading.

Hum No.	Basic Size	Trademark	Current Value
3/I	5-1/2"	TMK-1	$600
3/I	5-1/2"	TMK-2	$550
3/I	5-1/2"	TMK-3	$400
3/I	5-1/2"	TMK-4	$325
3/I	5-1/2"	TMK-5	$250
3/I	5-1/2"	TMK-6	$250
3/I	5-1/2"	TMK-7	$250
3/I	5-1/2"	TMK-8 TW	$200
3/II	8"	TMK-1	$1,300
3/II	8"	TMK-2	$1,175
3/II	8"	TMK-3	$700
3/II	8"	TMK-4	$650
3/II	8"	TMK-5	$525
3/II	8"	TMK-6 TW	$475
3/III	9-1/2"	TMK-1	$2,500
3/III	9-1/2"	TMK-2	$2,200
3/III	9-1/2"	TMK-3	$1,200
3/III	9-1/2"	TMK-4	$900
3/III	9-1/2"	TMK-5	$800
3/III	9-1/2"	TMK-6 TW	$800

Hum 3: Book Worm

Hum 4: Little Fiddler

This is the same design as Hum 2, Little Fiddler. The difference is that this is a smaller size than Hum 2. Another difference is that Hum 4 wears a black hat with an orange band, while Hum 2's hat is brown. The boy's vest, umbrella handle, and satchel handle sometimes can be found in yellow in TMK-1.

Hum 4: Little Fiddler

Hum No.	Basic Size	Trademark	Current Value
4 tilted head style			
	4-3/4"	TMK-1	$1,200
4	4-3/4"	TMK-1	$400
4	4-3/4"	TMK-2	$325
4	4-3/4"	TMK-3	$275
4	4-3/4"	TMK-4	$250
4	4-3/4"	TMK-5	$200
4	4-3/4"	TMK-6	$200
4	4-3/4"	TMK-7	$200
4	4-3/4"	TMK-8 CE	$200

Hum 5: Strolling Along

Hum 5 appears in only one basic size, 4-3/4". It was restyled in 1962, changing the position of the eyes.

Hum 5: Strolling Along

Hum No.	Basic Size	Trademark	Current Value
5	4-3/4"	TMK-1	$350
5	4-3/4"	TMK-2	$300
5	4-3/4"	TMK-3	$225
5	4-3/4"	TMK-4	$200
5	4-3/4"	TMK-5	$150
5	4-3/4"	TMK-6 CE	$150

Hum 6: Sensitive Hunter

The most notable variation is the shape of the suspenders on the boy's back. The suspenders form an "X" or "H." The "H" variation is found on all of the Crown Mark (TMK-1) figurines in the size 6 and 6/0. In the size 6/0, both styles of suspenders can be found in the TMK-3. The TMK-3 and up has the "X" style suspenders.

Hum No.	Basic Size	Trademark	Current Value
6/2/0	4"	TMK-6	$125
6/2/0 TW	4"	TMK-7	$125
6 CE	4-3/4"	TMK-1	$600 in "H" style
6/0	4-3/4"	TMK-1	$600
6/0	4-3/4"	TMK-2	$400 seldom seen in "X" style
6/0	4-3/4"	TMK-3	$325 either style
6/0	4-3/4"	TMK-4	$300
6/0	4-3/4"	TMK-5	$200
6/0	4-3/4"	TMK-6	$200
6/0	4-3/4"	TMK-7	$175
6/0 TW	4-3/4"	TMK-8	$150
6/I	5-1/2"	TMK-1	$700
6/I	5-1/2"	TMK-2	$550
6/I	5-1/2"	TMK-3	$325
6/I	5-1/2"	TMK-4	$300
6/I	5-1/2"	TMK-5	$200
6/I	5-1/2"	TMK-6 TW	$200
6/II	7-1/2"	TMK-1	$1,200 seen only in "X" style
6/II	7-1/2"	TMK-2	$875
6/II	7-1/2"	TMK-3	$500
6/II	7-1/2"	TMK-4	$475
6/II	7-1/2"	TMK-5	$400
6/II	7-1/2"	TMK-6 TW	$300

Hum 6: Sensitive Hunter

Hum 7: Merry Wanderer

This same design also appears as Hum 11 but in a smaller size. The Merry Wanderer is probably found in more sizes and variations than any other single figure in the collection. The Merry Wanderer is also the company's iconic motif and is used on all correspondence.

Hum No.	Basic Size	Trademark	Current Value
7/0	6-1/4"	TMK-1	$300
7/0	6-1/4"	TMK-2	$250
7/0	6-1/4"	TMK-3	$225
7/0	6-1/4"	TMK-4	$225
7/0	6-1/4"	TMK-5	$200
7/0	6-1/4"	TMK-6	$200
7/0	6-1/4"	TMK-7	$200
7/0	6-1/4"	TMK-7 CE	$200
Made for Little Switzerland			
7/0	6-1/4"	TMK-8 CE	$200
7/I	7"	TMK-1	$700 step base 7/I
	7"	TMK-2	$650 step base
7/I	7"	TMK-3	$600 step base 7/I
	7"	TMK-3	$500 standard base 7/I
	7"	TMK-4	$450
7/I	7"	TMK-5	$375
7/I	7"	TMK-6	$275
7/I	7"	TMK-7 TW	$200
7/I	7"	TMK-7 CE	$200 Expressions of Youth
7/II	9-1/2"	TMK-1	$1,200
7/II	9-1/2"	TMK-2	$800
7/II	9-1/2"	TMK-3	$700
7/II	9-1/2"	TMK-4	$700
7/II	9-1/2"	TMK-5	$600

Hum 7:
Merry Wanderer

Hum No.	Basic Size	Trademark	Current Value
7/II	9-1/2"	TMK-6	$600
7/II	9-1/2"	TMK-7 TW	$600
7/III	11-1/4"	TMK-1	$2,500
7/III	11-1/4"	TMK-2	$1,900
7/III	11-1/4"	TMK-3	$1,300
7/III	11-1/4"	TMK-4	$1,200
7/III	11-1/4"	TMK-5	$1,000
7/III	11-1/4"	TMK-6 TW	$1,000
7/X	32"	TMK-5	$12,000
7/X	32"	TMK-6	$10,000
7/X	32"	TMK-7	$9,000
7/X	32"	TMK-8	$25,000 retail

Hum 8: Book Worm

This figure is the same as Hum 3/I, except smaller.

Hum 8: Book Worm: a comparison between the normal skin coloration (left) and the pale coloration on the doll face piece. The left bears a Stylized Bee Mark (TMK-3). The one on the right is a doll face piece with a Double Crown Mark (TMK-1).

Hum No.	Basic Size	Trademark	Current Value
8	4"	TMK-1	$300
8	4"	TMK-2	$275
8	4"	TMK-3	$225
8	4"	TMK-4	$225
8	4"	TMK-5	$200
8	4"	TMK-6	$200
8	4"	TMK-7	$200
8	4"	TMK-8 TW	$200

Hum 9: Begging His Share

Begging His Share was originally designed to be a candleholder. It was originally called Congratulatory Visit. The cake occasionally can be found without a hole for the candle, but in TMK-3 it was changed to a solid cake. It can be found with and without the candle-holding hole in the cake in TMK-3. In 1964, the hole was eliminated when the figurine was remodeled.

Hum 9: Begging His Share

Hum No.	Basic Size	Trademark	Current Value
9	5-1/2"	TMK-1	$550
9	5-1/2"	TMK-2	$450
9	5-1/2"	TMK-3	$400 with hole in cake
9	5-1/2"	TMK-3	$300 without hole in cake 9
	5-1/2"	TMK-4	$225
9	5-1/2"	TMK-5	$175
9	5-1/2"	TMK-6	$150
9	5-1/2"	TMK-7 TW	$150

Hum 10: Flower Madonna

This piece was listed in early catalogs as Virgin With Flowers and Sitting Madonna with Child. Several color and mold variations are known for this figure. In the 10/I and 10/III sizes, it appears in color and in white over-glaze. The color cloak figurines, other than the powder blue (which is found in all trademarks), are found only in trademarks 1 and 2. Some of the cloak colors found are: tan, beige, ivory, brown, yellow, orange, and royal blue. An open-style or "doughnut" type halo is found in the Crowns and TMK-2s. The figure was remodeled in the mid-1950s, eliminating the hole in the halo (closed halo).

Hum No.	Basic Size	Trademark	Current Value
10/I	8 1/2 to 9-1/2"	TMK-1	$500 open halo
10/I	9-1/2"	TMK-2	$450 open halo
10/I	8"	TMK-3	$375 remaining closed halos
10/I	8"	TMK-4	$375
10/I	8"	TMK-5	$275
10/I	8"	TMK-6	$200
10/I TW	8"	TMK-7	$200
10/I TW	8"	TMK-7	$225
50th Anniversary in white only			
10/III	12 3/4"	TMK-1	$800 open halo
10/III	12 3/4"	TMK-2	$725 open halo
10/III	11-1/4"	TMK-3	$600 remaining closed halos
10/III	11-1/4"	TMK-4	$575
10/III	11-1/4"	TMK-5	$475
10/III TW	11-1/4"	TMK-6	$375

Hum 10: Flower Madonna

Hum 11: Merry Wanderer

Hum 11 is the same style as Hum 7. Although most of these figures have a five-button vest, zero-, four-, six-, and seven-button versions have been found. The button variations are found in the 11, 11/0, and 11/2/0 variations, but only in trademarks 1, 2, and 3.

Hum No.	Basic Size	Trademark	Current Value
11	4-3/4"	TMK-1	$575
11/2/0	4-1/4"	TMK-1	$375
11/2/0	4-1/4"	TMK-2	$275
11/2/0	4-1/4"	TMK-3	$250
11/2/0	4-1/4"	TMK-4	unknown if exists
11/2/0	4-1/4"	TMK-5	$100
11/2/0	4-1/4"	TMK-6	$125
11/2/0	4-1/4"	TMK-7	$100
11/2/0	4-1/4"	TMK-8	$100
11/2/0	4-1/4"	TMK-8	$150
Goebel 1871-2001 commemorative with Hummelscape			
11/2/0	4-1/4"	TMK-8	$189 retail
11/0	4-3/4"	TMK-1	$550
11/0	4-3/4"	TMK-2	$400
11/0	4-3/4"	TMK-3	$325
11/0	4-3/4"	TMK-4	unknown if exists
11/0	4-3/4"	TMK-5	$225
11/0	4-3/4"	TMK-6	$200
11/0	4-3/4"	TMK-7	$175
11/0	4-3/4"	TMK-7	$200
Special with red satchel, produced for Little Switzerland.			
11/0	4 3/4"	TMK-8+1	$339 retail
70th Anniversary with tag LE 1935			

Hum 11: Merry Wanderer

Hum 12: Chimney Sweep

When first introduced, this figure was called Smoky. It has had several minor restylings through the years.

Hum No.	Basic Size	Trademark	Current Value
12/4/0	3"	TMK-8	$99 retail
12/2/0	4"	TMK-2	$200
12/2/0	4"	TMK-3	$175
12/2/0	4"	TMK-4	$150
12/2/0	4"	TMK-5	$100
12/2/0	4"	TMK-6	$100
12/2/0	4"	TMK-7	$100
12/2/0	4"	TMK-8	$159 retail
12	6"	TMK-1	$450
12	6"	TMK-2	$375
12/I	5-1/2"	TMK-1	$450
12/I	5-1/2"	TMK-2	$375
12/I	5-1/2"	TMK-3	$275
12/I	5-1/2"	TMK-4	$275
12/I	5-1/2"	TMK-5	$200
12/I	5-1/2"	TMK-6	$200
12/I	5-1/2"	TMK-7	$200
12/I	5-1/2"	TMK-8+1	$379 retail 70th Anniversary with tag

Hum 12: Chimney Sweep

Hum 13: Meditation

The Hum 13/0 and the Hum 13/II sizes of Meditation were the first to be released in 1935. The piece was also called Little Messenger. The most significant variations are with regard to the flowers in the baskets. When first released, 13/II had flowers in the basket. Flowers are found in TMK-1, 2, and 3. The piece was restyled with no flowers in the basket in TMK-5. Some Crowns and Full Bee models of the figurine sported short pigtails with a painted red ribbon. Others had a red ribbon in a bow. Others had the pigtail on her left side flat against her face. Later the pigtails became prominent by sticking out from her face.

Hum No.	Basic Size	Trademark	Current Value
13/4/0	3-1/4"	TMK-8	$99 retail
13/2/0	4-1/4"	TMK-2	$200
13/2/0	4-1/4"	TMK-3	$200
13/2/0	4-1/4"	TMK-4	$175
13/2/0	4-1/4"	TMK-5	$150
13/2/0	4-1/4"	TMK-6 TW	$150
13/0	5	TMK-1	$475
13/0	5"	TMK-2	$400
13/0	5	TMK-3	$375
13/0	5"	TMK-4	$375
13/0	5"	TMK-5	$225
13/0	5"	TMK-6	$225
13/0	5"	TMK-7 TW	$225
13	7"	TMK-1	unknown value
13/I	5 1/4"	TMK-1	unknown value
13/II	7"	TMK-1	$2,000 with flowers
13/II	7"	TMK-2	$1,750 with flowers

Hum 13: Meditation

Hum No.	Basic Size	Trademark	Current Value
13/II	7"	TMK-3	$1,225 with flowers
13/II	7"	TMK-5	$275
13/II	7"	TMK-6 TW	$250
13/II	7"	TMK-8	$350
Revival Collection LE 2,000			
13/V	13-3/4"	TMK-1	$2,750
13/V	13-3/4"	TMK-2	$2,250
13/V	13-3/4"	TMK-3	$1,000
13/V	13-3/4"	TMK-4	$850
13/V	13-3/4"	TMK-5	$675
13/V	13-3/4"	TMK-6	$700
13/V	13-3/4"	TMK-7	$700
13/V	13-3/4"	TMK-8	$1,500 retail

14/A and Hum 14/B:
Book Worm Bookends

Two figures—a boy and a girl—make up this pair of bookends. The girl is the same as Hum 3 and 8, except the pictures in the book are in black and white instead of in color. Early marketed boy pieces were titled Learned Man. Typically the bookends were sold as a pair, but sometimes the boy was sold separately.

Hum No.	Basic Size	Trademark	Current Value
14 (Boy)	5-1/2"	TMK-1	$600-$800
14/A&B	5-1/2"	TMK-1	$800
14/A&B	5-1/2"	TMK-2	$475
14/A&B	5-1/2"	TMK-3	$400
14/A&B	5-1/2"	TMK-4	$400
14/A&B	5-1/2"	TMK-5	$400
14/A&B	5-1/2"	TMK-6 TW	$350
14/A&B	5-1/2"	TMK-7 TW	$350 Danbury Mint
14A	5-1/2	TMK-8+1	$389 retail
70th Anniversary Collection with tag LE of 1935			
14B	5-1/2	TMK-8+1	$389 retail
70th Anniversary Collection with tag LE of 1935			

70th Anniversary Collection pieces come with wooden stand.

Hum 14/A and Hum 14/B: Book Worms bookends

Hum 15: Hear Ye, Hear Ye

This figure was first called Night Watchman and remained so until around 1950. Two variations have been found. The time on the watch hanging from his coat shows various times. Gloves with fingers can be found on older figurines, or as mittens with no fingers depicted. Figurines with gloves with fingers are more elusive.

Hum No.	Basic Size	Trademark	Current Value
15/2/0	4"	TMK-6	$125
15/2/0	4"	TMK-7	$125
15/2/0	4"	TMK-8 CE	$199 retail
15/0	5"	TMK-1	$350
15/0	5"	TMK-2	$250
15/0	5"	TMK-3	$200
15/0	5"	TMK-4	$200
15/0	5"	TMK-5	$175
15/0	5"	TMK-6	$175
15/0	5"	TMK-7	$150
15/0	5"	TMK-8 CE	$175 Progression Set
15/0	5"	TMK-8	$339 retail
70th Anniversary with tag LE 1935			
15/I	6"	TMK-1	$500
15/I	6"	TMK-2	$450
15/I	6"	TMK-3	$350
15/I	6"	TMK-4	$350
15/I	6"	TMK-5	$250
15/I	6"	TMK-6	$250
15/I	6"	TMK-7 CE	$150
15/II	7-1/2"	TMK-1	$650
15/II	7-1/2"	TMK-2	$575
15/II	7-1/2"	TMK-3	$475

Hum 15: Hear Ye, Hear Ye

Hum No.	Basic Size	Trademark	Current Value
15/II	7-1/2"	TMK-4	$300
15/II	7-1/2"	TMK-5	$250
15/II	7-1/2"	TMK-6	$275
15/II	7-1/2"	TMK-7 CE	$150
15/II	7-1/2"	TMK-7 CE	$300
German employees Christmas figurine			
15/II	7-1/2"	TMK-7 CE	$250 Expressions of Youth

Hum 16: Little Hiker

Little Hiker was released in the 16/I and 16/2/0 sizes and was originally referred to as Happy-Go-Lucky. Early painting samples have been found with a green jacket and blue hat.

Hum No.	Basic Size	Trademark	Current Value
16/2/0	4-1/4"	TMK-1	$275
16/2/0	4-1/4"	TMK-2	$200
16/2/0	4-1/4"	TMK-3	$175
16/2/0	4-1/4"	TMK-4	$160
16/2/0	4-1/4"	TMK-5	$150-$160
16/2/0	4-1/4"	TMK-6	$150
16/2/0	4-1/4"	TMK-7	$140
16/2/0	4-1/4"	TMK-8 CE	$145 with "Final Issue" backstamp
16	5-1/2"	TMK-1	$475
16	5-1/2"	TMK-2	$400
16/I	5-1/2"	TMK-1	$475
16/I	5-1/2"	TMK-2	$400-$500
16/I	5-1/2"	TMK-3	$300
16/I	5-1/2"	TMK-4	$275
16/I	5-1/2"	TMK-5	$200
16/I	5-1/2"	TMK-6	$200
16/I TW	5-1/2"	TMK-7	$175

Hum 16: Little Hiker

Hum 17: Congratulations

Congratulations was first modeled with no socks. The figurine was restyled in 1971, with socks, new hair, and a textured finish. A variation with the handle of the horn pointing to the back instead of to the front has been found.

Hum 17: Congratulations

Hum No.	Basic Size	Trademark	Current Value
17/0	6"	TMK-1	$500 no socks
17/0	6"	TMK-2	$350 no socks
17/0	6"	TMK-3	$300 no socks
17/0	6"	TMK-4	$275 no socks
17/0	6"	TMK-5	$250 socks
17/0	6"	TMK-6	$225
17/0 CE	6"	TMK-7	$200 with "Final Issue" backstamp
17/2	8-1/4"	TMK-1	$2,000
17/2	8-1/4"	TMK-2	$1,750
17/2	8-1/4"	TMK-3	$1,500

Hum 18: Christ Child

Originally called Christmas Night, this figure is very similar to the Christ Child figure used in the Nativity Sets, Hum 214 and 260.

Hum 18: Christ Child

Hum No.	Basic Size	Trademark	Current Value
18	3-3/4" x 6-1/2"	TMK-1	$250
18	3-3/4" x 6-1/2"	TMK-2	$225
18	3-3/4" x 6-1/2"	TMK-3	$175
18	3-1/4" x 6"	TMK-4	$200
18	3-1/4" x 6"	TMK-5	$150
18	3-1/4" x 6"	TMK-6	$125
18	3-1/4" x 6"	TMK-7 TW	$125

Hum 19: Prayer Before Battle

Until 1986, when one of these ashtrays surfaced in the United States, it was thought this was a closed number and the piece was never produced. Even though one was found, it may well be the only one ever made.

Hum No.	Basic Size	Trademark	Current Value
19	5-1/2"	TMK-1	$5,000-$10,000

Hum 20: Prayer Before Battle

This piece has been listed at 4" and 4-1/2" in the price lists over the years. The colors of the flag typically have white on top and blue on the bottom. Occasionally these can be found reversed. In the first three trademarks, the horn can be found in several variations. Some will have a deep hole in the end of the horn; on others it will be painted to look like a hole. The handle of the horn can be found pointing up or down. Pointing down is the norm. The horn can also be found missing entirely.

Hum No.	Basic Size	Trademark	Current Value
20	4-1/4"	TMK-1	$450
20	4-1/4"	TMK-2	$375
20	4-1/4"	TMK-3	$300-$350
20	4-1/4"	TMK-4	$250
20	4-1/4"	TMK-5	$200
20	4-1/4"	TMK-6	$200
20	4-1/4"	TMK-7	$200
20	4-1/4"	TMK-8	$219 retail
20	4-1/4"	TMK-8	$259 retail 70th Anniversary with tag LE 1935

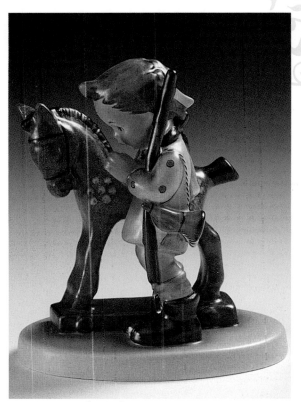

Hum 20: Prayer Before Battle

Hum 21: Heavenly Angel

This piece was first known as the Little Guardian or Celestial. The 21/0 size was the first to be introduced. It was followed by the larger sizes soon after. This is the same motif used on the famous 1971 annual plate, Hum 264.

Hum No.	Basic Size	Trademark	Current Value
21/0	4-1/4"	TMK-1	$300
21/I	4-1/4"	TMK-2	$225
21/0	4-1/4"	TMK-3	$175
21/0	4-1/4"	TMK-4	$170
21/0	4-1/4"	TMK-5	$125
21/0	4-1/4"	TMK-6	$100
21/0	4-1/4"	TMK-7	$159 retail
21/0/1/2	6"	TMK-1	$450
21/0/1/2	6"	TMK-2	$425
21/0/1/2	6"	TMK-3	$350
21/0/1/2	6"	TMK-4	$300
21/0/1/2	6"	TMK-5	$275
21/0/1/2	6"	TMK-6	$275
21/0/1/2	6"	TMK-7	$250
21/0/1/2	6"	TMK-8	$299 retail
21/I	6-3/4"	TMK-1	$475
21/I	6-3/4"	TMK-2	$450
21/I	6-3/4"	TMK-3	$375
21/I	6-3/4"	TMK-4	$350
21/I	6-3/4"	TMK-5	$275
21/I	6-3/4"	TMK-6	$225
21/I	6-3/4"	TMK-7 TW	$200
21/II	8-3/4"	TMK-1	$800
21/II	8-3/4"	TMK-2	$700

Hum 21: Heavenly Angel

Hum No.	Basic Size	Trademark	Current Value
21/II	8-3/4"	TMK-3	$600
21/II	8-3/4"	TMK-4	$500
21/II	8-3/4"	TMK-5	$375
21/II	8-3/4"	TMK-6	$350
21/II	8-3/4"	TMK-7 TW	$300
21/II	8-3/4"	TMK-7 TW	$225

Expressions of Youth

Hum 22: Angel With Bird

This holy water font, sometimes known as Seated Angel With Bird or Sitting Angel, has two variations in bowl design: with or without a lip on the back of the bowl. The larger size can be found also with eyes open or closed. There are several color variations on the tree, flowers, and bird.

Hum 22: Angel With Bird
holy water font

Hum No.	Basic Size	Trademark	Current Value
22	3-1/8" x 4-1/2"	TMK-1	$250
22/0	2-3/4" x 3-1/2"	TMK-1	$225
22/0	2-3/4" x 3-1/2"	TMK-2	$150
22/0	2-3/4" x 3-1/2"	TMK-3	$75
22/0	2-3/4" x 3-1/2"	TMK-4	$75
22/0	2-3/4" x 3-1/2"	TMK-5	$50
22/0	2-3/4" x 3-1/2"	TMK-6	$50
22/0	2-3/4" x 3-1/2"	TMK-7	$50
22/0	2-3/4" x 3-1/2"	TMK-8	$50
22/I	3-1/4" x 4-7/8"	TMK-1	$275
22/I	3-1/4" x 4-7/8"	TMK-2	$225
22/I	3-1/4" x 4-7/8"	TMK-3 CE	$175

Hum 23: Adoration

Known in the early years as Ave Maria and At the Shrine, Adoration was originally released in the smaller size. Soon after came the 23/III variation. Early trademarks have rounded corners on the base while the newer ones are more square. The TMK-1 in size 23/I frequently does not have flowers on the base.

Hum No.	Basic Size	Trademark	Current Value
23/I	6-1/4"	TMK-1	$600
23/I	6-1/4"	TMK-2	$550
23/I	6-1/4"	TMK-3	$475
23/I	6-1/4"	TMK-4	$400
23/I	6-1/4"	TMK-5	$350
23/I	6-1/4"	TMK-6	$325
23/I	6-1/4"	TMK-7	$250
23/I	6-1/4"	TMK-8	$250
23	9"	TMK-1	$900
23/III	9"	TMK-1	$900
23/III	9"	TMK-2	$850
23/III	9"	TMK-3	$825
23/III	9"	TMK-4	$700
23/III	9"	TMK-5	$625
23/III	9"	TMK-6	$600
23/III	9"	TMK-7	$575

Hum 23: Adoration

Hum 24: Lullaby

This candleholder's former name was Cradle Song. Variations can be found in the size and construction of the hole for the candle.

Hum 24: Lullaby candleholder

Hum No.	Basic Size	Trademark	Current Value
24/I	3-1/4" x 5"	TMK-1	$400
24/I	3-1/4" x 5"	TMK-2	$350
24/I	3-1/4" x 5"	TMK-3	$250
24/I	3-1/4" x 5"	TMK-4	$250
24/I	3-1/4" x 5"	TMK-5	$175
24/I	3-1/4" x 5"	TMK-6	$150
24/I	3-1/4" x 5"	TMK-7 TW	$150
24/I	3-1/4" x 5"	TMK-7	$279 retail
70th Anniversary with tag LE 1935			
24/III	6" x 8-3/4"	TMK-1	$900
24/III	6" x 8-3/4"	TMK-2	$875
24/III	6" x 8-3/4"	TMK-3	$550
24/III	6" x 8-3/4"	TMK-4	$500
24/III	6" x 8-3/4"	TMK-5	$450
24/III	6" x 8-3/4"	TMK-6 TW	$425

Hum 25: Angelic Sleep

This candleholder was called Angel's Joy in some early company literature.

Hum 25: Angelic Sleep candleholder

Hum No.	Basic Size	Trademark	Current Value
25	3-1/2" x 5"	TMK-1	$450
25	3-1/2" x 5"	TMK-2	$375
25	3-1/2" x 5"	TMK-3	$250
25	3-1/2" x 5"	TMK-4	$200
25	3-1/2" x 5"	TMK-5	$175
25	3-1/2" x 5"	TMK-6 TW	$150

Hum 26: Child Jesus

The color of the robe is normally a deep orange-red. A significant variation has appeared in the Stylized Bee (TMK-3) 26/0 size, in which the robe has also been found as either light blue or green. The bowl on this font is fluted on the top edge. The Crown trademark can be found with and without a lip on the back edge of the bowl. Later trademarks have the lip.

Hum 26: Child Jesus holy water font

Hum No.	Basic Size	Trademark	Current Value
26/0	2-3/4" x 5"	TMK-1	$250
26/0	2-3/4" x 5"	TMK-2	$125
26/0	2-3/4" x 5"	TMK-3	$75
26/0	2-3/4" x 5"	TMK-4	$50
26/0	2-3/4" x 5"	TMK-5	$40
26/0	2-3/4" x 5"	TMK-6	$40
26/0	2-3/4" x 5"	TMK-7	$40
26	3" x 5-3/4"	TMK-1	$450
26/I	3-1/4" x 6"	TMK-1	$300
26/I	3-1/4" x 6"	TMK-2	$275
26/I	3-1/4" x 6"	TMK-3	$250

Hum 27: Joyous News

This figurine is hard to find in good condition in trademarks 1 and 2 in the 27/III size. The horn is found broken on many of these pieces. The smaller size (27/I) was made as a candleholder and is very difficult to find.

Hum 27: Joyous News

Hum No.	Basic Size	Trademark	Current Value
27/I	2-3/4"	TMK-1	$575
27/I	2-3/4"	TMK-2	$500
27/III	4-1/4" x 4-3/4"	TMK-1	$750
27/III	4-1/4" x 4-3/4"	TMK-2	$700
27/III	4-1/4" x 4-3/4"	TMK-3	$675
27/III	4-1/4" x 4-3/4"	TMK-5	$275
27/III	4-1/4" x 4-3/4"	TMK-6	$250
27/III	4-1/4" x 4-3/4"	TMK-7	$225

Hum 28: Wayside Devotion

This figurine has been called The Little Shepherd and Evensong over the years. (Hum 99: Eventide is the same figurine but is smaller and without the shrine.)

Hum No.	Basic Size	Trademark	Current Value
28/II	7"	TMK-1	$900
28/II	7"	TMK-2	$750
28/II	7"	TMK-3	$600
28/II	7"	TMK-4	$500
28/II	7"	TMK-5	$350
28/II	7"	TMK-6	$300
28/II	7"	TMK-7	$275
28/II	7"	TMK-8	$475 retail
28	8-3/4"	TMK-1	$1,100
28/III	8-3/4"	TMK-1	$1,000
28/III	8-3/4"	TMK-2	$850
28/III	8-3/4"	TMK-3	$800
28/III	8-3/4"	TMK-4	$700
28/III	8-3/4"	TMK-5	$550
28/III	8-3/4"	TMK-6	$500
28/III	8-3/4"	TMK-7 TW	$400

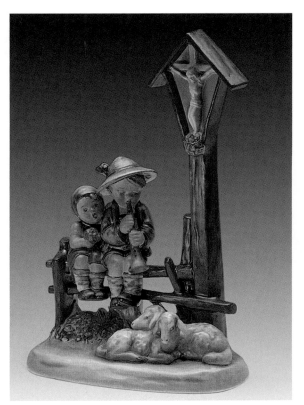

Hum 28: Wayside Devotion

Hum 29: Guardian Angel

This figure was first modeled in two sizes. A similar piece, Hum 248, is considered to be a redesign of Hum 29. The wings are frequently found broken on this figurine.

Hum 29: Guardian Angel holy water font

Hum No.	Basic Size	Trademark	Current Value
29	2-3/4" x 6"	TMK-1 CE	$1,225
29/0	2-1/2" x 5-5/8"	TMK-1	$1,100
29/0	2-1/2" x 5-5/8"	TMK-2	$900
29/0	2-1/2" x 5-5/8"	TMK-3 CE	$800
29/I	3" x 6-3/8"	TMK-1	$1,400
29/I	3" x 6-3/8"	TMK-2 CE	$1,200

Hum 30/A and Hum 30/B: Ba-Bee Rings

These wall plaques were first called Hummel Rings. The rings were sold as a set and are priced as such. Figures with the rings painted red in the Crown (TMK- 1) era are found in both sizes. The red ring figures are very difficult to find and have a blue hair ribbon instead of orange.

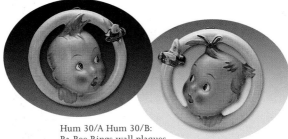

Hum 30/A Hum 30/B:
Ba-Bee Rings wall plaques

Hum No.	Basic Size	Trademark	Current Value
30/0 A&B	4-3/4" x 5"	TMK-1	$400
30/0 A&B	4-3/4" x 5"	TMK-1	$3,500 red rings
30/0 A&B	4-3/4" x 5"	TMK-2	$350
30/0 A&B	4-3/4" x 5"	TMK-3	$275
30/0 A&B	4-3/4" x 5"	TMK-4	$275
30/0 A&B	4-3/4" x 5"	TMK-5	$225
30/0 A&B	4-3/4" x 5"	TMK-6	$225
30/0 A&B	4-3/4" x 5"	TMK-7	$220
30/0 A&B	4-3/4" x 5"	TMK-8	$200
30/I A&B	5-1/4" x 6"	TMK-1	$1400
30/1 A&B	5-1/4" x 6"	TMK-1	$3,700 red rings

Hum 31: Advent Group

This candleholder was often called Advent Group or Silent Night With White Child or Silent Night With Black Child. Both versions have been found in the Crown Mark (TMK-1) only. They are considered to be very rare. The number produced has never been determined.

Hum 31: Advent Group candleholder

Hum No.	Basic Size	Trademark	Current Value
31	3-1/2" x 5"	TMK-1	$12,000 black child
31	3-1/2" x 5"	TMK-1	$12,000 white child

Hum 32: Little Gabriel

When first released, this figure was called Joyous News. The size designator for the 32/0 version was dropped in TMK-5 and had only the 32 thereafter. The first two trademarks of the larger 6" also had the 32 designator. Little Gabriel was redesigned in 1982.

Hum 32: Little Gabriel

Hum No.	Basic Size	Trademark	Current Value
32/0	5"	TMK-1	$450
32/0	5"	TMK-2	$400
32/0	5"	TMK-3	$275
32/0	5"	TMK-4	$250
32/0	5"	TMK-6	$175
32	5"	TMK-5	$175
32	5"	TMK-6	$150
32	5"	TMK-7 TW	$150
32	6"	TMK-1	$1,300
32	6"	TMK-2	$1,100
32/I	6"	TMK-1	$1,200
32/I	6"	TMK-2	$1,000
32/I	6"	TMK-3	$900

Hum 33: Joyful

This ashtray utilizes a figure very similar to Hum 53: Joyful, with the addition of a small bird on the edge of the tray next to the figurine. Typically, the figure wears a blue dress and orange shoes, but a variation with the colors switched—orange dress and blue shoes—has been found (trademark unknown).

Hum 33: Joyful Ashtray

Hum No.	Basic Size	Trademark	Current Value
33	3-1/2" x 6"	TMK-1	$350
33	3-1/2" x 6"	TMK-2	$300
33	3-1/2" x 6"	TMK-3	$225
33	3-1/2" x 6"	TMK-4	$200
33	3-1/2" x 6"	TMK-5	$125
33	3-1/2" x 6"	TMK-6	$125

Hum 34: Singing Lesson

This ashtray utilizes a figure very similar to Hum 64, with the addition of a small bird perched on the edge.

Hum 34: Singing Lesson ashtray

Hum No.	Basic Size	Trademark	Current Value
33	3-1/2" x 6"	TMK-1	$350
33	3-1/2" x 6"	TMK-2	$300
33	3-1/2" x 6"	TMK-3	$225
33	3-1/2" x 6"	TMK-4	$200
33	3-1/2" x 6"	TMK-5	$125
33	3-1/2" x 6"	TMK-6 TW	$125

Hum 35: Good Shepherd

Hum 35 in the Crown trademark can be found with yellow lambs and green grass. This font also has a flared bowl. A lip is found on TMK-2 and up.

Hum 35:
Good Shepherd
holy water font

Hum No.	Basic Size	Trademark	Current Value
35/0	2-1/4" x 4-3/4"	TMK-1	$200
35/0	2-1/4" x 4-3/4"	TMK-2	$150
35/0	2-1/4" x 4-3/4"	TMK-3	$75
35/0	2-1/4" x 4-3/4"	TMK-4	$70
35/0	2-1/4" x 4-3/4"	TMK-5	$50
35/0	2-1/4" x 4-3/4"	TMK-6	$50
35/0	2-1/2" x 4-3/4"	TMK-7	$50
35/0	2-1/2" x 4-3/4"	TMK-8	$50
35	2-1/4" x 4-3/4"	TMK-1 TW	$350 yellow lambs and green grass
35	2-1/4" x 4-3/4"	TMK-1 TW	$300
35/I	2-3/4" x 5-3/4"	TMK-1	$300
35/I	2-3/4" x 5-3/4"	TMK-2	$225
35/I	2-3/4" x 5-3/4"	TMK-3 TW	$175

Hum 36: Child With Flowers

This holy water font has been called Flower Angel and Angel With Flowers. There have been only minor variations in the colors of the font. TMK-2 and up are found with a lip on the back of the bowl.

Hum 36:
Child With Flowers
holy water font

Hum No.	Basic Size	Trademark	Current Value
36/0	3 1/2" x 4-1/2"	TMK-1	$150
36/0	3 1/2" x 4-1/2"	TMK-2	$100
36/0	3 1/2" x 4-1/2"	TMK-3	$75
36/0	3 1/2" x 4-1/2"	TMK-4	$75
36/0	3 1/2" x 4-1/2"	TMK-5	$50
36/0	3 1/2" x 4-1/2"	TMK-6	$50
36/0	3-1/2" x 4-1/2"	TMK-7	$50
36/0	3-1/2" x 4-1/2"	TMK-8	$50
36.	3-1/2" x 4-1/2"	TMK-1 CE	$200
36/I	3-1/2" x 4-1/2"	TMK-1	$200
36/I	3-1/2" x 4-1/2"	TMK-2	$175
36/I	3-1/2" x 4-1/2"	TMK-3 CE	$150

Hum 37: Herald Angels

This piece is a group of figures very similar to Hum 38, 39, and 40, placed together on a common round base with a candle receptacle in the center. There are two versions: low and high candleholder. The higher holder is found on the older pieces. TMK-3 can be found in the low or high candleholder.

Hum 37: Herald Angels candleholder

Hum No.	Basic Size	Trademark	Current Value
37	2-1/2" x 4"	TMK-1	$300
37	2-1/2" x 4"	TMK-2	$275
37	2-1/2" x 4"	TMK-3	$250
37	2-1/2" x 4"	TMK-4	$225
37	2-1/2" x 4"	TMK-5	$175
37	2-1/2" x 4"	TMK-6	$150

Hum 38, Hum 39, and Hum 40: Angel Trio

These three figures—Joyous News Angel With Lute, Joyous News Angel With Accordion, and Joyous News Angel With Trumpet—are presented as a set of three. These pieces have been called Little Heavenly Angels and Angel Trio in old company literature. They each come in three versions according to size and candle size.

Hum No.	Basic Size	Trademark	Current Value
I/38/0	2" x 2-1/2"	TMK-1	$150-$200
I/38/0	2" x 2-1/2"	TMK-2	$100-$125
I/38/0	2" x 2-1/2"	TMK-3	$95-$100
I/38/0	2" x 2-1/2"	TMK-4	$85-$95
I/38/0	2" x 2-1/2"	TMK-5	$80-$85
I/38/0	2" x 2-1/2"	TMK-6	$75-$80
I/38/0	2" x 2-1/2"	TMK-7	$70-$75
I/38/0	2" x 2-1/2"	TMK-8 TW	$70
III/38/0	2" x 2-1/2"	TMK-1	$150-$200
III/38/0	2" x 2-1/2"	TMK-2	$100-$125
III/38/0	2" x 2-1/2"	TMK-3	$90-$100
III/38/0	2" x 2-1/2"	TMK-4	$80-$90
III/38/0	2" x 2-1/2"	TMK-5	$70-$80
III/38/0	2" x 2-1/2"	TMK-6 TW	$60-$70
III/38/1	2-1/2" x 2-3/4"	TMK-1	$300-$350
III/38/1	2-1/2" x 2-3/4"	TMK-2	$250-$300
III/38/1	2-1/2" x 2-3/4"	TMK-3	$200-$250
I/39/0	2" x 2-1/2"	TMK-1	$150-$200
I/39/0	2" x 2-1/2"	TMK-2	$105-$125
I/39/0	2" x 2-1/2"	TMK-3	$95-$105

Hum 38, Hum 39, and Hum 40:
Angel Trio candleholders

Hum No.	Basic Size	Trademark	Current Value
I/39/0	2" x 2-1/2"	TMK-4	$85-$95
I/39/0	2" x 2-1/2"	TMK-5	$80-$85
I/39/0	2" x 2-1/2"	TMK-6	$75-$80
I/39/0	2" x 2-1/2"	TMK-7	$70-$75
I/39/0	2" x 2-1/2"	TMK-8 TW	$70
III/39/0	2" x 2-1/2"	TMK-1	$150-$200
III/39/0	2" x 2-1/2"	TMK-2	$100-$125
III/39/0	2" x 2-1/2"	TMK-3	$90-$100
III/39/0	2" x 2-1/2"	TMK-4	$80-$90
III/39/0	2" x 2-1/2"	TMK-5	$70-$80
III/39/0	2" x 2-1/2"	TMK-6	$60-$70
III/39/1	2-1/2" x 2-3/4"	TMK-1	$300-$350
III/39/1	2-1/2" x 2-3/4"	TMK-2	$250-$300
III/39/1	2-1/2" x 2-3/4"	TMK-3 TW	$200-$250
I/40/0	2" x 2-1/2"	TMK-1	$150-$200
I/40/0	2" x 2-1/2"	TMK-2	$105-$125
I/40/0	2" x 2-1/2"	TMK-3	$95-$105
I/40/0	2" x 2-1/2"	TMK-4	$85-$95
I/40/0	2" x 2-1/2"	TMK-5	$80-$85
I/40/0	2" x 2-1/2"	TMK-6	$75-$80
I/40/0	2" x 2-1/2"	TMK-7	$70-$75
I/40/0	2" x 2-1/2"	TMK-8 TW	$70
III/40/0	2" x 2-1/2"	TMK-1	$150-$200
III/40/0	2" x 2-1/2"	TMK-2	$100-$125
III/40/0	2" x 2-1/2"	TMK-3	$90-$100
III/40/0	2" x 2-1/2"	TMK-4	$80-$90
III/40/0	2" x 2-1/2"	TMK-5	$70-$80
III/40/0	2" x 2-1/2"	TMK-6	$60-$70
III/40/1	2-1/2" x 2-3/4"	TMK-1	$300-$350
III/40/1	2-1/2" x 2-3/4"	TMK-2	$250-$300
III/40/1	2-1/2" x 2-3/4"	TMK-3	$200-$250

Hum 41: Singing Lesson

This figure had been listed as a closed number, but the existence of the piece is now substantiated. Details are not known, but the piece is said to be similar to Singing Lesson (Hum 63) without the base. There are no known examples, but samples in this category have turned up from time to time. Collector value is $3,000-$7,000.

Hum 42: Good Shepherd

Good Shepherd has been found with the decimal point designator in the 42 mold number. There are two very rare variations: a blue gown rather than the normal brownish-red color, and a white gown with blue stars. This is found on the 42/0 size in the Crown (TMK-1) and Full Bee (TMK-2) figures.

Hum No.	Basic Size	Trademark	Current Value
42/0	6-1/4"	TMK-1	$450-$600
42/0	6-1/4"	TMK-2	$280-$430
42/0	6-1/4"	TMK-3	$225-$430
42/0	6-1/4"	TMK-4	$275-$325
42/0	6-1/4"	TMK-5	$275-$300
42/0	6-1/4"	TMK-6	$195-$225
42/0	6-1/4"	TMK-7	$195-$225
42/I	7-1/4" x 8"	TMK-3	$2,600-$4,000
42/I	7-1/2"	TMK-1	$4,200-$5,500
42/I	7-1/2"	TMK-2	$3,600-$4,500

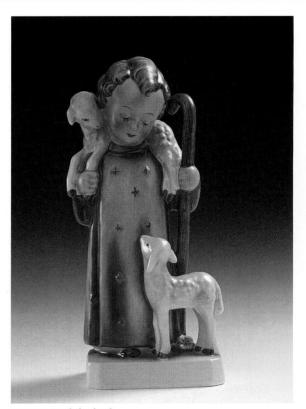

Hum 42: Good Shepherd

Hum 43: March Winds

This figurine has been called Urchin in old company catalogs. There appear to be two slightly different designs. In the earlier pieces, the boy looks more toward the rear than in the newer ones, but there are no significant variations to be found.

Hum 43: March Winds

Hum No.	Basic Size	Trademark	Current Value
43/5/0	2-3/4"	TMK-7	$55
43	5"	TMK-1	$250-$400
43	5"	TMK-2	$165-$225
43	5"	TMK-3	$160-$200
43	5"	TMK-4	$160-$175
43	5"	TMK-5	$125-$190
43	5"	TMK-6	$125-$190
43	4-3/4" x 5-1/2"	TMK-7	$115-$150
43	4-3/4" x 5-1/2"	TMK-8	$199 retail

Hum 44/A: Culprits and
Hum 44/B: Out of Danger

Both of these lamps are about 8-1/2" tall. There are no significant variations that would affect the collector value of either one; only minor changes such as the location of the switch.

Hum No.	Basic Size	Trademark	Current Value
44	8-1/2" to 9-1/2"	TMK-1	$390-$450
44/A	8-1/2" to 9-1/2"	TMK-1	$300-$390
44/A	8-1/2" to 9-1/2"	TMK-2	$260-$288
44/A	8-1/2" to 9-1/2"	TMK-3	$240-$288
44/A	8-1/2"	TMK-4	$225-$240
44/A	8-1/2"	TMK-5	$195-$230
44/A	8-1/2"	TMK-6	$200-$250
44/B	8-1/2" to 9-1/2"	TMK-1	$300-$390
44/B	8-1/2" to 9-1/2	TMK-2	$260-$300
44/B	8-1/2" to 9-1/2	TMK-3	$240-$260
44/B	8-1/2"	TMK-4	$225-$260
44/B	8-1/2"	TMK-5	$210-$250
44/B	8-1/2"	TMK-6	$195-$230

Hum 44/A: Culprits table lamp

Hum 44/B:
Out of Danger table lamp

Hum 45: Madonna With Halo and
Hum 46: Madonna Without Halo

These Madonnas are often confusing to collectors because of their similarity. Sometimes the mold number appears on the wrong piece. At least nine legitimate variations have been found. The chief differences are in size, color, and glaze treatment.

Hum No.	Basic Size	Trademark	Value (White)	Value (Color)
45/0	10-1/2"	TMK-1	$75 -$120	$120-$165
45/0	10-1/2"	TMK-2	$55-$100	$60-$110
45/0	10-1/2"	TMK-3	$45-$85	$45-$85
45/0	10-1/2"	TMK-4	$30-$50	$45-$60
45/0	10-1/2"	TMK-5	$25-$45	$45-$50
45/0	10-1/2"	TMK-6	$20-$45	$45-$50
45/I	11-1/2" to 13-1/4"	TMK-1	$90-$120	$180-$240
45/I	11-1/2" to 13-1/4"	TMK-2	$60-$90	$105-$180
45/I	11-1/2" to 13-1/4"	TMK-3	$55-$60	$99-$105
45/I	11-1/2" to 13-1/4"	TMK-4	$55-$60	$95-$105
45/I	11-1/2" to 13-1/4"	TMK-5	$50-$60	$90-$105
45/I	11-1/2" to 13-1/4"	TMK-6	$45-$60	$90-$105
45/I	11-1/2" to 13-1/4"	TMK-7	$45-$60	$70-$105
45/I	11-1/2" to 13-1/4"	TMK-8	$45-$60	$60-$105

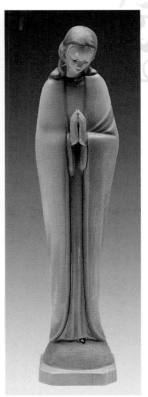

Hum 45: Madonna With Halo   Hum 46: Madonna Without Halo

Hum No.	Basic Size	Trademark	Value (White)	Value (Color)
45/III	16-1/4"	TMK-1	$150-$210	$240-$360
45/III	16-1/4"	TMK-2	$105-$180	$165-$225
45/III	16-1/4"	TMK-3	$105-$140	$105-$140
45/III	16-1/4"	TMK-4	$70-$85	$99-$120
45/III	16-1/4"	TMK-5	$65-$70	$99-$120
45/III	16-1/4"	TMK-6	$40-$70	$99-$165
46/0	10-1/4"	TMK-2	$55-$85	$120-$165
46/0	10-1/4"	TMK-3	$35-$40	$55-$85
46/0	10-1/4"	TMK-4	$35-$55	$40-$70
46/0	10-1/4"	TMK-5	$25-$45	$40-$65
46/0	10-1/4"	TMK-6	$25-$45	$40-$60
46/I	11-1/4"	TMK-1	$180-$240	$180-$240
46/I	11-1/4"	TMK-2	$105-$135	$105-$135
46/I	11-1/4"	TMK-3	$95-$105	$95-$105
46/I	11-1/4"	TMK-4	$90-$100	$90-$100
46/I	11-1/4"	TMK-5	$85-$95	$85-$95
46/I	11-1/4"	TMK-6	$80-$95	$80-$95
46/III	16"	TMK-1	$150-$210	$240-$360
46/III	16"	TMK-2	$105-$185	$165-$225
46/III	16"	TMK-3	$85-$140	$105-$130
46/III	16"	TMK-4	$70-$85	$95-$120
46/III	16"	TMK-5	$70-$85	$95-$110
46/III	16"	TMK-6	$70-$80	$90-$115

Hummel® Listings

Hum 177: School Girls

The listings that follow reflect a range of prices that span all known trademarks and sizes. Generally speaking, the lower the trademark number, the higher the value.

The year listed reflects the approximate date of an item's initial year of production. Keep in mind that some pieces were designed years before they were introduced into the line, which accounts for sample pieces with earlier trademarks.

All pieces are figurines unless otherwise noted.

For more specific information and individual pricing based on trademark variations, please consult *The Official M.I. Hummel® Price Guide* by Heidi von Recklinghausen (Krause Publications, 2010).

Hum 47: Goose Girl   Hum 48: Madonna wall plaque

Hum No./Name	Year	Trademarks	Value
Hum 47: Goose Girl	1936	1-8	$120-$780
Hum 48: Madonna plaque	1936	1-6	$55-$1,200
Hum 49: To Market	1936	1-8	$110-$1,020
Hum 50: Volunteers	1936	1-8	$140-$900
Hum 51: Village Boy	1936	1-8	$55-$690
Hum 52: Going to Grandma's	1936	1-8	$150-$960
Hum 53: Joyful	1936	1-4, 6-7	$85-$270
Hum III/53: Joyful candy box	1936, 1964	1-7	$120-$510
Hum 54: Silent Night candleholder	1936	1-7	$220-$9,000
Hum 55: Saint George	1936	1-7	$210-$1,800
Hum 56/A: Culprits and Hum 56/B: Out of Danger	1936	1-8	$210-$665

Hum 49: To Market

Hum 50: Volunteers

Hum 51: Village Boy

Hum No./Name	Year	Trademarks	Value
Hum 57: Chick Girl	1936	1-8	$110-$630
Hum III/57: Chick Girl candy box	N/A	1-7	$105-$510
Hum 58: Playmates	1936	1-8	$115-$600
Hum III/58: Playmates candy box	N/A	1-7	$105-$510
Hum 59: Skier	1936	1-8	$140-$515
Hum 60/A: Farm Boy and Hum 60/B: Goose Girl bookends	N/A	1-6	$250-$760
Hum 61/A: Playmates and Hum 61/B: Chick Girl bookends	N/A	1-6	$250-$760
Hum 62: Happy Pastime ashtray	1936	1-6	$95-$390
Hum 63: Singing Lesson	1937	1-8	$90-$300
Hum III/63: Singing Lesson candy box	N/A	1-7	$105-$510
Hum 64: Shepherd's Boy	1937	1-8	$170-$1,200

Hum 52: Going To Grandma's

Hum 53: Joyful

Hum 54: Silent Night Candleholder

Hum 55: Saint George

Hum 56/A: Culprits

Hum 56/B: Out of Danger

Hum 57: Chick Girl

Hum 58: Playmates

Hum 59: Skier

Hum 62: Happy Pastime ashtray

Hum 63: Singing Lesson

Hum 64: Shepherd's Boy

FINAL ISSUE
LETZTE AUSGABE
1993

Hum 65: Farewell

Hum 66: Farm Boy   Hum 67: Doll Mother

Hum No./Name	Year	Trademarks	Value
Hum 65: Farewell	1937	1-7	$170-$4,800
Hum 66: Farm Boy	1937	1-8	$170-$540
Hum 67: Doll Mother	1937	1-8	$150-510
Hum 68: Lost Sheep	1937	1-7	$99-$460
Hum 69: Happy Pastime	1937	1-7	$115-$390
Hum III/69: Happy Pastime candy box	N/A	1-6	$120-$510
Hum 70: Holy Child	1937	1-7	$170-$510
Hum 71: Stormy Weather	1937	1-8	$210-$785
Hum 72: Spring Cheer	1937	1-6	$120-$390
Hum 73: Little Helper	1937	1-8	$85-$300
Hum 74: Little Gardener	1937	1-8	$90-$450
Hum 75: White Angel holy water font	1937	1-7	$30-$165

Hum 68: Lost Sheep

Hum 69: Happy Pastime

Hum 71: Stormy Weather

Hum 72: Spring Cheer

Hum 73: Little Helper

Hum 74: Little Gardener

Hum 76/A: Doll Mother bookend

Hum 75: White Angel holy water font

Hum 78: Blessed Child

Hum 77: Cross With Doves holy water font

Hum 79: Globe Trotter. Rear view shows different basket weave pattern variations. The older version is on the left.

Hum 80: Little Scholar   Hum 81: School Girl

Hum No./Name	Year	Trademarks	Value
Hum 76/A: Doll Mother and Hum 76/B: Prayer Before Battle bookends	N/A	1	$6,000-$9,000
Hum 77: Cross With Doves holy water font	1937	1	$3,000-$6,000
Hum 78: Blessed Child	1937	1-8	$25-$600
Hum 79: Globe Trotter	1937	1-7	$120-$450
Hum 80: Little Scholar	1937	1-8	$135-$480
Hum 81: School Girl	1937	1-8	$105-$420
Hum 82: School Boy	1938	1-8	$105-$960
Hum 83: Angel Serenade With Lamb	1938	1-7	$165-$450
Hum 84: Worship	1938	1-8	$115-$1,800
Hum 85: Serenade	Late 1930s	1-8	$70-$925

Hum 83: Angel Serenade With Lamb

Hum 84: Worship

Hum 85: Serenade

Hum 86: Happiness

Hum No./Name	Year	Trademarks	Value
Hum 86: Happiness	Late 1930s	1-8	$95-$300
Hum 87: For Father	Late 1930s	1-8	$165-$480
Hum 88: Heavenly Protection	Late 1930s	1-8	$315-$960
Hum 89: Little Cellist	1938	1-8	$155-$1,025
Hum 90/A: Eventide and Hum 90/B: Adoration bookends	N/A	N/A	$3,000-$9,000
Hum 91/A and Hum 91/B: Angel at Prayer holy water font	N/A	1-8	$65-$300
Hum 92: Merry Wanderer plaque	1938	1-6	$90-$345
Hum 93: Little Fiddler plaque	1938	1-6	$90-$2,400
Hum 94: Surprise	Late 1930s	1-8	$105-$600
Hum 95: Brother	N/A	1-8	$145-$480
Hum 96: Little Shopper	Late 1930s	1-8	$105-$330
Hum 97: Trumpet Boy	1938	1-7	$90-$315

Hum 87: For Father

Hum 88: Heavenly Protection

Hum 89: Little Cellist

Hum 90/A and Hum 90/B: Eventide and Adoration bookends

Hum 91/A and 91/B: Angel at Prayer holy water font

Hum 92:
Merry Wanderer wall plaque

Hum 93:
Little Fiddler wall plaque

Hum 94: Surprise

Hum 95: Brother

Hum 96: Little Shopper

Hum 97: Trumpet Boy

Hum 98: Sister

Hum 99: Eventide

Hum No./Name	Year	Trademarks	Value
Hum 98: Sister	1938	1-8	$55-$420
Hum 99: Eventide	Late 1930s	1-7	$220-$2,100
Hum 100: Shrine table lamp	1938	1-2	$4,800-$6,000
Hum 101: To Market table lamp	1937	1-3	$300-$6,000
Hum 102: Volunteers table lamp	1937	1	$4,800-$6,000
Hum 103: Farewell table lamp	1937	1	$4,800-$6,000
Hum 104: Eventide table lamp	1938	1	$4,800-$6,000
Hum 105: Adoration With Bird	N/A	1	$4,200-$4,800
Hum 106: Merry Wanderer plaque	1938	1	$1,800-$2,400
Hum 107: Little Fiddler plaque	1938	1	$1,800-$2,400
Hum 108: Angel With Two Children at Feet plaque	1938	1-2	$1,500-$9,000
Hum 109: Happy Traveler	1938	1-8	$105-$900
Hum 110: Let's Sing	Late 1930s	1-8	$110-$360

Hum 105: Adoration With Bird

Hum 107:
Little Fiddler wall plaque

Hum 108: Angel With Two
Children at Feet wall plaque
in relief

Hum 109: Happy Traveler

Hum 110: Let's Sing

Hum III/110: Let's Sing candy box

Hum 111: Wayside Harmony

Hum 112: Just Resting

Hum 113:
Heavenly Song candleholder.
This is a rare porcelain-like figurine that may fall into the faience category. It has an incised Crown (TMK-1), but the incised MI Hummel signature is either too light to discern or is absent.

Hum 114: Let's Sing ashtray

Hum No./Name	Year	Trademarks	Value
Hum III/110: Let's Sing candy box	N/A	1-6	$120-$510
Hum 111: Wayside Harmony	1938	1-8	$110-$510
Hum II/111: Wayside Harmony table lamp	1950s	1-3	$230-$480
Hum 112: Just Resting	1938	1-8	$105-$510
Hum II/112: Just Resting table lamp	1950s	1-3	$225-$480
Hum 113: Heavenly Song candleholder	1938	1-3, 5	$1,800-$6,000
Hum 114: Let's Sing ashtray	1938	1-6	$90-$600

Hum 115:
Girl With Nosegay

Hum 116:
Girl With Fir Tree

Hum 117:
Boy With Horse

Hum No./Name	Year	Trademarks	Value
Hum 115: Girl With Nosegay; and Hum 116: Girl With Fir Tree; and Hum 117: Boy With Horse Advent Group candleholders	1938	1-8	$40-$150 ea.
Hum 118: Little Thrifty	Late 1930s	1-8	$110-$450
Hum 119: Postman	1939-40	1-8	$99-$450
Hum 120: Joyful and Let's Sing bookends	ca. 1939	1	$6,000-$12,000
Hum 121/A and B: Wayside Harmony and Just Resting bookends	ca. 1939	1	$3,000-$6,000 ea.
Hum 122: Puppy Love and Serenade With Dog bookends	ca. 1939	1	$6,000-$12,000

Hum 118: Little Thrifty

Hum 119: Postman

Hum 121:
Wayside Harmony bookend

Hum 122: Puppy Love bookend

Hum 123: Max and Moritz

Hum 124: Hello

Hum 125: Vacation Time wall plaque

Hum 126:
Retreat to Safety wall plaque

Hum 127: Doctor

Hum No./Name	Year	Trademarks	Value
Hum 123: Max and Moritz	1940	1-8	$155-$480
Hum 124: Hello	1939-40	1-8	$165-$600
Hum 125: Vacation Time plaque	N/A	1-7	$135-$450
Hum 126: Retreat to Safety plaque	1939	1-6	$110-$420
Hum 127: Doctor	1940	1-8	$110-$390
Hum 128: Baker	1939	1-8	$140-$450
Hum 129: Band Leader	1939	1-8	$140-$1,500
Hum 130: Duet	1939	1-7	$180-$2,100
Hum 131: Street Singer	1939	1-8	$140-$420
Hum 132: Star Gazer	1939	1-8	$150-$480
Hum 133: Mother's Helper	1939	1-8	$135-$420
Hum 134: Quartet plaque	1939-40	1-6	$150-$600
Hum 135: Soloist	1940	1-8	$30-$1,550

Hum 128: Baker

Hum 129: Band Leader

Hum 130: Duet

Hum 131: Street Singer

Hum 132: Star Gazer

Hum 133: Mother's Helper

Hum 134: Quartet wall plaque

Hum 135: Soloist

Hum 136: Friends

Hum 137/B:
Child in Bed wall plaque

Hum 138:
Tiny Baby in Crib wall plaque

Hum 139:
Flitting Butterfly wall plaque

Hum 140: The Mail is Here wall plaque

Hum 141: Apple Tree Girl

Hum 142: Apple Tree Boy

Hum 143: Boots

Hum No./Name	Year	Trademarks	Value
Hum 136: Friends	1940	1-8	$150-$9,000
Hum 137/A and Hum 137/B: Child in Bed plaques	1940	1-7	$40-$4,200
Hum 138: Tiny Baby in Crib plaque	1940	1-2	$1,200-$3,000
Hum 139: Flitting Butterfly plaque	1940	1-3, 5-7	$45-$1,500
Hum 140: The Mail is Here plaque	1940	1-6	$150-$900
Hum 141: Apple Tree Girl	1940	1-8	$105-$29,900
Hum 142: Apple Tree Boy	1940	1-8	$105-$29,900
Hum 143: Boots	1940	1-7	$140-$600
Hum 144: Angelic Song	1941	1-8	$105-$315
Hum 145: Little Guardian	1941	1-8	$105-$300

Hum 144: Angelic Song

Hum 145: Little Guardian

Hum 146:
Angel Duet holy water font

Hum 147:
Angel Shrine holy water font

Hum 150: Happy Days

Hum 151:
Madonna Holding Child

Hum No./Name	Year	Trademarks	Value
Hum 146: Angel Duet holy water font	1941	1-7	$35-$135
Hum 147: Angel Shrine holy water font	1941	1-8	$35-$165
Hum 148-149: Unknown			
Hum 150: Happy Days	N/A	1-8	$120-$960
Hum 151: Madonna Holding Child	N/A	1-2, 5-6	$240-$7,200
Hum 152/A: Umbrella Boy	1942	1-8	$279-$4,200
Hum 152/B: Umbrella Girl	Late 1940s	1-8	$329-$4,200
Hum 153: Auf Wiedersehen	1943	1-8	$170-$2,400
Hum 154: Waiter	1943	1-8	$150-$1,260
Hum 155: Madonna Holding Child	1943	1	N/A

Hum 152/A: Umbrella Boy

Hum 152/B: Umbrella Girl

Hum 153: Auf Wiedersehen

Hum 154: Waiter   Hum 155: Madonna Holding Child plaque.

Hum No./Name	Year	Trademarks	Value
Hum 156: Unknown			
Hum 157-162: Town Children	1943	N/A	N/A
Hum 163: Whitsuntide	1946	1-3, 5-7	$200-$750
Hum 164: Worship holy water font	1946	1-4, 6-8	$35-$180
Hum 165: Swaying Lullaby plaque	1946	1-3, 5-7	$120-$660
Hum 166: Boy With Bird ashtray	1946	1-6	$90-$390
Hum 167: Angel With Bird holy water font	Mid-1940s	1-8	$40-$180
Hum 168: Standing Boy plaque	1948	1-2, 3, 5-6	$120-$395
Hum 169: Duet	1945	1-8	$105-$330
Hum 170: School Boys	1943	108	$840-$3,000
Hum 171: Little Sweeper	1944	1-8	$70-$300

Hum 157
through
Hum 162:
"Town Children"

Hum 163: Whitsuntide

Hum 164:
Worship holy water font

Hum 165:
Swaying Lullaby wall plaque

Hum 166: Boy With Bird ashtray

Hum 167:
Angel With Bird holy water font

Hum 168: Standing Boy wall plaque

Hum 169: Bird Duet

Hum 170: School Boys

Hum 171: Little Sweeper

Hum 172/A & B: Festival Harmony (Angel With Mandolin) *Left & Center*
Hum 173: Festival Harmony (Angel With Flute) *Right*

Hum No./Name	Year	Trademarks	Value
Hum 172: Festival Harmony (Angel With Mandolin)	1947	1-7	$70-$2,100
Hum 173: Festival Harmony (Angel With Flute)	1947	1-7	$70-$2,100
Hum 174: She Loves Me, She Loves Me Not	1945	1-8	$145-$420
Hum 175: Mother's Darling	1945	1-7	$145-$480
Hum 176: Happy Birthday	1945	1-8	$165-$690
Hum 177: School Girls	1946	1-8	$840-$3,000
Hum 178: The Photographer	1948	1-8	$195-$660
Hum 179: Coquettes	1948	1-7	$195-$660
Hum 180: Tuneful Goodnight plaque	1946	1-6	$120-$720

Hum 174: She Loves Me, She Loves Me Not

Hum 175: Mother's Darling

Hum 176: Happy Birthday

Hum 177: School Girls

Hum 178: The Photographer

Hum 179: Coquettes

Hum 180:
Tuneful Goodnight wall plaque

Hum No./Name	Year	Trademarks	Value
Hum 181: Old Man Reading Newspaper	1948	N/A	$9,000-$12,000
Hum 182: Good Friends	1946	1-8	$140-$450
Hum 183: Forest Shrine	1946	1-3, 5-7	$240-$1,140
Hum 184: Latest News	1946	1-8	$205-$1,200
Hum 185: Accordion Boy	1947	1-4	$170-$450
Hum 186: Sweet Music	1947	1-8	$130-$900
Hum 187: Dealer Plaques and Display Plaques	1947	1-7	$70-$960
Hum 188: Celestial Musician	1948	1-8	$80-$1,200
Hum 189: Old Woman Knitting	1948	N/A	$9,000-$12,000
Hum 190: Old Woman Walking to Market	1948	N/A	$9,000-$12,000

Hum 182: Good Friends

Hum 181: Old Man Reading Newspaper

Hum 183: Forest Shrine

Hum 184: Latest News

Hum 185: Accordion Boy

Hum 186: Sweet Music

Hum 187: Display Plaque. *A special edition commemorating 100 years of service by the Army and Air Force Exchange Service (AAFES)*

Hum 188: Celestial Musician

Hum 189: Old Woman Knitting

Hum 190:
Old Woman Walking to Market

Hum No./Name	Year	Trademarks	Value
Hum 191: Old Man Walking to Market	1948	N/A	$9,000-$12,000
Hum 192: Candlelight candleholder	1948	1-7	$165-$1,080
Hum 193: Angel Duet candleholder	1948	1-7	$150-$1,080
Hum 194: Watchful Angel	1948	1-8	$240-$1,260
Hum 195: Barnyard Hero	1948	1-8	$130-$720
Hum 196: Telling Her Secret	1948	1-8	$180-$900
Hum 197: Be Patient	1948	1-8	$140-$600
Hum 198: From Market	1948	1-8	$120-$480
Hum 199: Feeding Time	1948	1-8	$135-$600
Hum 200: Little Goat Herder	1948	1-8	$140-$510
Hum 201: Retreat to Safety	1948	1-8	$130-$720

Hum 191:
Old Man Walking to Market

Hum 192:
Candlelight candleholder

Hum 193:
Angel Duet candleholder

Hum 194: Watchful Angel

Hum 195: Barnyard Hero

Hum 196: Telling Her Secret

Hum 197: Be Patient

Hum 198: Home From Market

Hum 199: Feeding Time

Hum 200: Little Goat Herder

Hum 201: Retreat to Safety

Hum 203: Signs of Spring   Hum 204: Weary Wanderer

Hum 205: German language dealer plaque

Hum 206:
Angel Cloud holy water font

Hum 207:
Heavenly Angel holy water font

Hum No./Name	Year	Trademarks	Value
Hum 202: Old Man Reading Newspaper table lamp	1948	N/A	$9,000-$12,000
Hum 203: Signs of Spring	1950	1-6	$135-$600
Hum 204: Weary Wanderer	1949	1-7	$170-$540
Hum 205: German Language Dealer Plaque or Display Plaque	1949	1-3	$510-$1,020
Hum 206: Angel Cloud holy water font	Early 1950s	1-7	$35-$300
Hum 207: Heavenly Angel holy water font	1949-Early 1950s	1-8	$35-$300
Hum 208: French Language Dealer Plaque	N/A	2-3	$1,800-$3,600

Hum 214: Nativity Set

Hum No./Name	Year	Trademarks	Value
Hum 209: Swedish Language Dealer Plaque	N/A	2	$2,400-$3,600
Hum 210: English Language Dealer Plaque	N/A	2	$12,000-$15,000
Hum 211: English Language Dealer Plaque	N/A	2	$12,000-$15,000
Hum 212: Orchestra	N/A	N/A	N/A
Hum 213: Spanish Language Dealer Plaque	N/A	2	$4,800-$6,000

Hum 217: Boy With Toothache

Hum 218: Birthday Serenade

Hum 219/2/0: Little Velma

Hum 220: We Congratulate

Hum 222: Madonna wall plaque

Hum 221: Happy Pastime candy box

Hum 226: The Mail is Here

Hum 224: Wayside Harmony table lamp

Hum 228: Good Friends table lamp

Hum 227: She Loves Me, She Loves Me Not table lamp

Hum 232: Happy Days table lamp

Hum 231: Birthday Serenade table lamp

Hum 236/A and Hum 236/B: No name

Hum No./Name	Year	Trademarks	Value
Hum 214: Nativity Set	1951	2-8	Values vary depending on piece
Hum 215-216: Unknown			
Hum 217: Boy With Toothache	1951	2-8	$150-$315
Hum 218: Birthday Serenade	1952	2-8	2-8
Hum 219/2/0: Little Velma	1952	2	$2,400-$3,600
Hum 220: We Congratulate	1952	2-8	$110-$345
Hum 221: Happy Pastime candy box	1952	N/A	$3,000-$6,000
Hum 222: Madonna plaque	1952	2-3	$450-$750
Hum 223: To Market table lamp	1950s	2-8	$300-$510
Hum 224: Wayside Harmony table lamp	1952	2-8	$210-$480

Hum 238/A: Angel With Lute, Hum 238/B: Angel With Accordion, and Hum 238/C: Angel With Trumpet (Angel Trio Set)

Hum 239/A: Girl With Nosegay, Hum 239/B: Girl With Doll, Hum 239/C: Boy With Horse, and Hum 239/D: Girl With Fir Tree

Hum No./Name	Year	Trademarks	Value
Hum 225: Just Resting table lamp	1952	2-8	$210-$480
Hum 226: The Mail is Here	1952	2-8	$365-$840
Hum 227: She Loves Me, She Loves Me Not table lamp	1953	2-6	$225-$510
Hum 228: Good Friends table lamp	1953	2-6	$225-$510
Hum 229: Apple Tree Girl table lamp	1953	2-6	$225-$600
Hum 230: Apple Tree Boy table lamp	1953	2-6	$225-$600
Hum 231: Birthday Serenade table lamp	N/A	2, 5-6	$300-$1,800
Hum 232: Happy Days table lamp	1954	2, 5-6	$255-$1,020
Hum 233: Unknown			
Hum 234: Birthday Serenade table lamp	N/A	2-6	$255-$1,260
Hum 235: Happy Days table lamp	1954	2-6	$270-$665
Hum 236/A and Hum 236/B: No Name	1954	2	$6,000-$9,000
Hum 237: Star Gazer plaque	1954	2	$6,000-$9,000
Hum 238/A: Angel With Lute, Hum 238/B: Angel With Accordion, and Hum 238/C: Angel With Trumpet angel trio set	1967	4-8	$40-$75
Hum 239/A: Girl With Nosegay, Hum 239/B: Girl With Doll, Hum 239/C: Boy With Horse, and Hum 239/D: Girl With Fir Tree	1960s	3-8	$40-$120

Hum 240: Little Drummer

Hum 241:
Angel Lights candleholder

Hum 242: Angel Joyous News
With Trumpet holy water font

Hum 243: Madonna and Child
holy water font

Hum 246:
Holy Family holy water font

Hum 248:
Guardian Angel holy water font

Hum 247: Standing Madonna With Child

Hum 249: Madonna and Child plaque in relief

Hum 250/A: Little Goat Herder and
Hum 250/B: Feeding Time bookends

Hum 251/A: Good Friends and
Hum 251/B: She Loves Me, She Loves Me Not bookends

Hum 252/A: Apple Tree Boy and
Hum 252/B: Apple Tree Girl bookends

Hum No./Name	Year	Trademarks	Value
Hum 240: Little Drummer	1950s	2-8	$105-$225
Hum 241: Joyous News, Angel With Lute holy water font	1955	2	$900-$1,200
Hum 241: Angel Lights candleholder	1978	5-6	$180-$300
Hum 242: Angel Joyous News With Trumpet holy water font	1955	2	$900-$1,200
Hum 243: Madonna and Child holy water font	1960s	2-8	$40-$180
Hum 244-245: Open Numbers			
Hum 246: Holy Family holy water font	1955	2-8	$40-$180
Hum 247: Standing Madonna With Child	1965	N/A	$6,000-$9,000
Hum 248: Guardian Angel holy water font	1958	3-7	$40-$900
Hum 249: Madonna and Child plaque	N/A	N/A	$6,000-$9,000
Hum 250/A: Little Goat Herder and Hum 250/B: Feeding Time bookends	1964	2-3, 5-6	$180-$450
Hum 251/A: Good Friends and Hum 251/B: She Loves Me, She Loves Me Not bookends	1964	2-3, 5-6	$180-$450
Hum 252/A: Apple Tree Boy and Hum 252/B: Apple Tree Girl bookends	1964	3, 5-6	$180-$255
Hum 253: Unknown			
Hum 254: Girl With Mandolin	1962	CN	$3,000-$6,000
Hum 255: A Stitch in Time	1964	3-7	$70-$480
Hum 256: Knitting Lesson	1963-64	3-7	$315-$665
Hum 257: For Mother	1963-64	3-8	$55-$525

Hum 255: A Stitch in Time

Hum 256: Knitting Lesson

Hum 257: For Mother

Hum 258: Which Hand?

Hum 260: Large nativity set

Hum No./Name	Year	Trademarks	Value
Hum 258: Which Hand?	1963-64	3-8	$140-$495
Hum 259: Girl With Accordion	1962	N/A	$6,000-$9,000
Hum 260: Nativity Set (large)	1968	4-6	Values vary depending on individual piece
Hum 261: Angel Duet	1968	4-8	$165-$510
Hum 262: Heavenly Lullaby	1968	4-7	$120-$515
Hum 263: Merry Wanderer plaque	1968	4	$6,000-$9,000
Hum 264-Hum 279, Hum 283-Hum 291: Annual Plates	Multiple	4-7	Values vary depending on individual plate

Hum 261: Angel Duet

Hum 262: Heavenly Lullaby

Hum 263:
Merry Wanderer plaque

Hum 300: Bird Watcher

Hum 301: Christmas Angel

Hum 302:
Concentration, a rare sample

Hum 303:
Arithmetic Lesson, a rare sample

Hum 304: The Artist

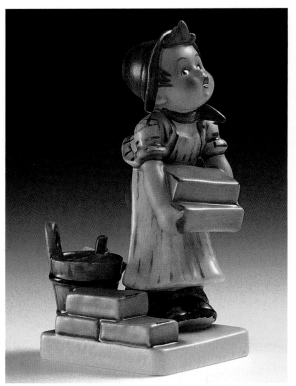

Hum 305: The Builder

Hum 306: Little Bookkeeper

Hum No./Name	Year	Trademarks	Value
Hum 280-282: Anniversary Plates	N/A	5-6	$60-$90 ea.
Hum 292-295: Friends Forever plate series	1991-92	7	$60-$90 ea.
Hum 296-299: Four Seasons plate series	1996	7	$100-$120 ea.
Hum 300: Bird Watcher	1979	2-8	$150-$3,000
Hum 301: Christmas Angel	1989	3, 6-8	$175-$3,000
Hum 302: Concentration	PFE	2	$2,400-$3,000
Hum 303: Arithmetic Lesson	PFA	2	$2,400-$3,000
Hum 304: The Artist	1970	2-8	$175-$3,000
Hum 305: The Builder	1955	2-8	$175-$3,000
Hum 306: Little Bookkeeper	1955	2-8	$200-$3,000
Hum 307: Good Hunting	1962	2-8	$170-$3,000
Hum 308: Little Tailor	1972	2-8	$175-$3,000
Hum 309: With Loving Greetings	1983	2-8	$125-$3,000
Hum 310: Searching Angel plaque	1979	2-7	$85-$1,800
Hum 311: Kiss Me	1961	2-8	$200-$3,000
Hum 312: Honey Lover	1955	2, 6-8	$140-$3,000
Hum 313: Sunny Morning	2003	2, 8	$319-$3,000
Hum 314: Confidentially	1972	2-7	$195-$3,000
Hum 315: Mountaineer	1964	2-8	$150-$3,000
Hum 316: Relaxation	1955	2, 8	$390-$3,000
Hum 317: Not For You	1961	2-8	$170-$3,000
Hum 318: Art Critic	1991	2, 6-7	$180-$3,000
Hum 319: Doll Bath	1962	2-8	$200-$3,000
Hum 320: The Professor	1991	2, 7-8	$145-$3,000
Hum 321: Wash Day	1955	2-8	$70-$3,000
Hum 322: Little Pharmacist	1955	2-8	$170-$3,000
Hum 323: Merry Christmas plaque	1979	2, 5-7	$85-$1,800

Hum 307: Good Hunting

Hum 308: Little Tailor

Hum 309: With Loving Greetings

Hum 310:
Searching Angel wall plaque

Hum 311: Kiss Me

Hum 312: Honey Lover

Hum 313: Sunny Morning

Hum 314: Confidentially

Hum 315: Mountaineer

Hum 316: Relaxation

Hum 317: Not For You

Hum 318: Art Critic

Hum 319: Doll Bath

Hum 320: The Professor

Hum 321: Wash Day

Hum No./Name	Year	Trademarks	Value
Hum 324: At the Fence	PFE	2	$2,400-$3,000
Hum 325: Helping Mother	PFE	2	$2,400-$3,000
Hum 326: Being Punished	PFE	2	$2,400-$3,000
Hum 327: The Run-a-way	1972	2-8	$175-$3,000
Hum 328: Carnival	1955	2-7	$145-$3,000
Hum 329: Off to School	PFE	2-3	$1,800-$3,000
Hum 330: Baking Day	1985	2-7	$180-$3,000
Hum 331: Crossroads	1955	2-8	$285-$3,000
Hum 332: Soldier Boy	1963	2-7	$150-$3,000
Hum 333: Blessed Event	1964	2-8	$230-$3,000
Hum 334: Homeward Bound	1971	2-7	$220-$3,000
Hum 335: Lucky Boy	1995	2-3, 7	$115-$3,000
Hum 336: Close Harmony	Early 1960s	2-8	$215-$3,000
Hum 337: Cinderella	1972	2-6	$200-$3,000

Hum 322: Little Pharmacist

Hum 323:
Merry Christmas wall plaque

Hum 324: At the Fence, a rare sample

Hum 325: Helping Mother,
a rare sample

Hum 327: The Run-a-way

Hum 328: Carnival

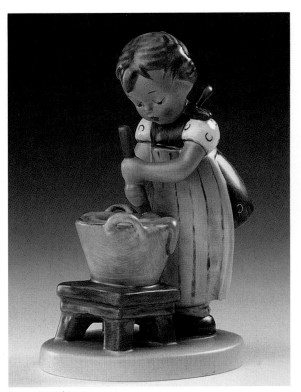

Hum 330: Baking Day

Hum 331: Crossroads

Hum 332: Soldier Boy

Hum No./Name	Year	Trademarks	Value
Hum 338: Birthday Cake	1989	2-3, 6-7	$100-$3,000
Hum 339: Behave!	1956	2-3, 7-8	$270-$6,000
Hum 340: Letter to Santa Claus	1971	2-8	$235-$12,000
Hum 341: Birthday Present	1956	2-4, 7-8	$105-$3,000
Hum 342: Mischief Maker	1972	2-7	$185-$3,000
Hum 343: Christmas Song	1981	2-8	$95-$5,000
Hum 344: Feathered Friends	1972	2-8	$200-$3,000
Hum 345: A Fair Measure	1962	2-7	$195-$3,000
Hum 346: Smart Little Sister	1962	2-8	$170-$3,000
Hum 347: Adventure Bound	1971	2, 4-8	$2,400-$9,000
Hum 348: Ring Around the Rosie	1960	2-8	$1,725-$9,000
Hum 349: Florist	2003	2-4, 8	$300-$3,000
Hum 350: On Holiday	1981	3-8	$110-$3,000
Hum 351: The Botanist	1982	4-8	$69-$1,800

Hum 333: Blessed Event

Hum 334: Homeward Bound

Hum 335: Lucky Boy

Hum 336: Close Harmony

Hum 337: Cinderella

Hum 338: Birthday Cake candleholder

Hum 339: Behave!

Hum 340: Letter to Santa Claus

Hum 341: Birthday Present

Hum 342: Mischief Maker

Hum 343: Christmas Song

Hum 344: Feathered Friends

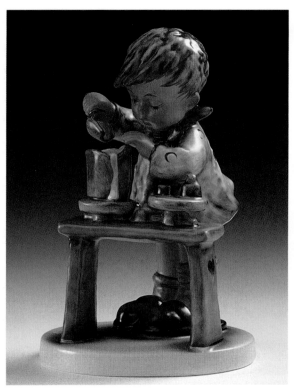

Hum 345: A Fair Measure

Hum 346: Smart Little Sister

Hum 347: Adventure Bound

Hum 348: Ring Around the Rosie

Hum 349: Florist

Hum 350: On Holiday   Hum 351: The Botanist

Hum No./Name	Year	Trademarks	Value
Hum 352: Sweet Greetings	1981	4-8	$125-$3,000
Hum 353: Spring Dance	1964	3-8	$225-$3,000
Hum 354/A: Angel With Lantern, Hum 354/B: Angel With Trumpet, and Hum 354/C: Angel With Bird holy water fonts	N/A	N/A	N/A
Hum 355: Autumn Harvest	1972	3-8	$145-$1,800
Hum 356: Gay Adventure	1971-72	3-8	$140-$1,800
Hum 357: Guiding Angel	1972	4-8	$70-$135
Hum 358: Shining Light	1972	4-8	$70-$135
Hum 359: Tuneful Angel	1972	4-8	$70-$135
Hum 360/A: Boy and Girl, Hum 360/B: Boy, and Hum 360/C: Girl wall vases	1959	3, 5-6	$85-$450 ea.
Hum 361: Favorite Pet	1964	2-8	$195-$3,000

Hum 352: Sweet Greetings

Hum 353: Spring Dance

Hum 354/A: Angel With Lantern

Hum 354/B: Angel With Trumpet and
Hum 354/C: Angel With Bird holy water fonts

Hum 355: Autumn Harvest   Hum 356: Gay Adventure

Hum 357: Guiding Angel, Hum 358: Shining Light, and
Hum 359: Tuneful Angel

Hum 360/C: Girl,
Hum 360/B: Boy, and
Hum 360/A: Boy and Girl
wall vases

Hum 361: Favorite Pet

Hum 362: Forget Me Not
(early sample)

Hum 363: Big Housecleaning

Hum No./Name	Year	Trademarks	Value
Hum 362: Forget Me Not	1959	2-5	$600-$3,000
Hum 363: Big Housecleaning	1972	2-7	$190-$5,300
Hum 364: Supreme Protection	1984	4-6	$210-$2,400
Hum 365: Hummele	1999	4, 8	$90-$1,800
Hum 366: Flying Angel	1963	4-8	$95-$165
Hum 367: Busy Student	1964	3-8	$120-$600
Hum 368: Lute Song	PFE	4	$1,200-$1,800
Hum 369: Follow the Leader	1972	3-8	$780-$3,000
Hum 370: Companions	PFE	3-5	$1,200-$5,000
Hum 371: Daddy's Girls	1989	4-8	$165-$2,400
Hum 372: Blessed Mother	PFE	4	$1,800-$2,400
Hum 373: Just Fishing	1985	4-7	$165-$2,400
Hum 374: Lost Stocking	1972	3-8	$110-$2,400
Hum 375: Morning Stroll	1994	4, 7-8	$130-$2,400

Hum 365: Hummele

Hum 366: Flying Angel

Hum 367: Busy Student

Hum 369: Follow the Leader

Hum 371: Daddy's Girls

Hum 373: Just Fishing

Hum 374: Lost Stocking

Hum 375: Morning Stroll

Hum 376: Little Nurse

Hum 377: Bashful

Hum 378: Easter Greetings

Hum 380: Daisies Don't Tell

Hum 381: Flower Vendor   Hum 382: Visiting an Invalid

Hum No /Name	Year	Trademarks	Value
Hum 376: Little Nurse	1982	4-8	$175-$2,400
Hum 377: Bashful	1966	4-8	$140-$2,400
Hum 378: Easter Greetings	1966	4-7	$140-$2,400
Hum 379: Don't Be Shy	PFE	3-4	$1,800-$3,000
Hum 380: Daisies Don't Tell	1981	4-6	$165-$2,400
Hum 381: Flower Vendor	1972	4-8	$180-$2,400
Hum 382: Visiting an Invalid	1972	4-7	$135-$900
Hum 383: Going Home	1985	4-8	$230-$2,400
Hum 384: Easter Time	1972	4-8	$175-$900
Hum 385: Chicken-Licken	1972	4-8	$70-$900
Hum 386: On Secret Path	1972	4-8	$175-$900
Hum 387: Valentine Gift	1977	4-5	$285-$4,500
Hum 388: Little Band candleholder	1967	4-6	$150-$270

Hum 383: Going Home

Hum 384: Easter Time

Hum 385: Chicken-Licken

Hum 386: On Secret Path

Hum 387: Valentine Gift

Hum 388: Little Band candleholder

Hum No./Name	Year	Trademarks	Value
Hum 388/M: Little Band candleholder and music box	N/A	4-6	$240-$300
Hum 389-391: Little Band			
Hum 389: Girl With Sheet Music	1968	4-8	$65-$165
Hum 390: Boy With Accordion	1968	4-8	$65-$165
Hum 391: Girl With Trumpet	1968	4-8	$65-$165
Hum 392: Little Band	1968	4-6	$165-$270
Hum 392/M: Little Band music box	N/A	4-6	$240-$300
Hum 393: Dove holy water font	PFE	4	$1,200-$1,800
Hum 394: Timid Little Sister	1981	5-8	$300-$2,400

Hum 388/M: Little Band candleholder and music box

Little Band Hum 389: Girl With Sheet Music

Little Band Hum 390: Boy With Accordion

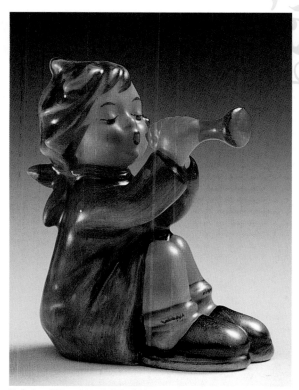

Little Band Hum 391: Girl With Trumpet

Hum 392/M: Little Band music box

Hum No./Name	Year	Trademarks	Value
Hum 395: Shepherd Boy	1996	5, 7-8	$170-$2,400
Hum 396: Ride Into Christmas	1972	4-8	$165-$1,500
Hum 397: The Poet	1994	4, 7-8	$90-$2,400
Hum 398: Spring Bouquet	PFE	5	$1,800-$2,400
Hum 399: Valentine Joy	1980	5-6	$150-$4,500
Hum 400: Well Done!	PFE	5	$1,800-$2,400
Hum 401: Forty Winks	1973	5	$319-$2,400
Hum 402: True Friendship	2002	5, 8	$399-$2,400

Hum 394: Timid Little Sister

Hum 395: Shepherd Boy

Hum 396: Ride Into Christmas

Hum 397: The Poet

Hum 399: Valentine Joy

Hum 401: Forty Winks

Hum 402: True Friendship

Hum 403: An Apple a Day

Hum 404: Sad Song   Hum 405: Sing With Me

Hum No./Name	Year	Trademarks	Value
Hum 403: An Apple a Day	1989	5-8	$99-$2,400
Hum 404: Sad Song	2005	5, 8	$295-$2,400
Hum 405: Sing With Me	1985	5-8	$199-$2,400
Hum 406: Pleasant Journey	1987	5-6	$1,650-$3,600
Hum 407: Flute Song	PFE	5	$1,800-$2,400
Hum 408: Smiling Through	1985	5-6	$210-$3,000
Hum 409: Coffee Break	1984	5-6	$180-$2,400
Hum 410: Little Architect	1993	5, 7-8	$205-$2,400
Hum 411: Do I Dare?	2006	5, 8	$149-$2,400
Hum 412: Bath Time	1990	5-8	$300-$2,400
Hum 413: Whistler's Duet	1991	5-7	$190-$2,400
Hum 414: In Tune	1981	508	$195-$2,400
Hum 415: Thoughtful	1981	5-8	$165-$2,400

Hum 406: Pleasant Journey

Hum 408: Smiling Through

Hum 409: Coffee Break

Hum 410: Little Architect

Hum 411: Do I Dare?

Hum 412: Bath Time

Hum 413: Whistler's Duet

Hum 414: In Tune

Hum 415: Thoughtful

Hum 416: Jubilee

Hum 418: What's New?

Hum 420: Is It Raining?

Hum 421: It's Cold

Hum No./Name	Year	Trademarks	Value
Hum 416: Jubilee	1985	6	$300-$360
Hum 417: Where Did You Get That?	PFE	N/A	N/A
Hum 418: What's New?	1990	6-8	$200-$235
Hum 419: Good Luck	PFE	N/A	N/A
Hum 420: Is It Raining?	1989	6-8	$195-$369
Hum 421: It's Cold	1981	6, 8	$99-$240
Hum 422: What Now?	1981	6	$210-$240
Hum 423: Horse Trainer	1990	6-8	$160-$268
Hum 424: Sleep Tight	1990	6-8	$160-$255
Hum 425: Pleasant Moment	2007	8	$429
Hum 426: Pay Attention	1999	6-8	$110-$1,200
Hum 427: Where Are You?	1999	6-8	$110-$1,200
Hum 428: Summertime Surprise	1997	6-8	$95-$1,800

Hum 422: What Now?

Hum 423: Horse Trainer

Hum 424: Sleep Tight

Hum 426: Pay Attention

Hum 427: Where Are You?

Hum 428: Summertime Surprise

Hum 429: Hello World

Hum 430: In D Major

Hum 432: Knit One, Purl One

Hum 431: The Surprise

Hum 433: Sing Along

Hum 434: Friend or Foe?   Hum 435: Delicious

Hum No./Name	Year	Trademarks	Value
Hum 429: Hello World	1989	6-7	$180-$240
Hum 430: In D Major	1989	6-8	$145-$160
Hum 431: The Surprise	1988	6	$180-$1,800
Hum 432: Knit One, Purl One	1983	6-8	$85-$179
Hum 433: Sing Along	1987	6-7	$185-$205
Hum 434: Friend or Foe?	1991	6-8	$160-$255
Hum 435: Delicious	1996	6-8	$105-$1,800
Hum 436: An Emergency	2007	8	$400
Hum 437: Tuba Player	1989	6-8	$190-$345
Hum 438: Sounds of the Mandolin	1988	6-8	$95-$170
Hum 439: A Gentle Glow candleholder	1987	6-7	$115-$150

Hum 436: An Emergency   Hum 437: Tuba Player

Hum No./Name	Year	Trademarks	Value
Hum 440: Birthday Candle candleholder	1983	6	$210-$240
Hum 441: Call to Worship clock	1988	6	$840-$900
Hum 442: Chapel Time clock	1986	6	$1,050-$1,800
Hum 443: Country Song	PFE	N/A	N/A
Hum 444-445: Open Numbers			
Hum 446: A Personal Message	PFE	N/A	N/A
Hum 447: Morning Concert	1984	6	$150-$180
Hum 448: Children's Prayer	PFE	N/A	N/A
Hum 449: The Little Pair	1990	6-8	$130-$240
Hum 450: Will It Sting?	2000	6, 8	$260-$1,800
Hum 451: Just Dozing	1995	7-8	$155-$279
Hum 452: Flying High Christmas ornament	1988	6	$105-$180

Hum 438: Sounds of the Mandolin

Hum 439: A Gentle Glow candleholder

Hum 440:
Birthday Candle candleholder

Hum 441: Call to Worship clock

Hum 442: Chapel Time clock

Hum 447: Morning Concert

Hum 449: The Little Pair

Hum 450: Will It Sting?   Hum 451: Just Dozing

Hum No./Name	Year	Trademarks	Value
Hum 453: The Accompanist	1988	6-8	$70-$135
Hum 454: Song of Praise	1988	6-8	$70-$135
Hum 455: The Guardian	1991	6-8	$110-$200
Hum 456: Sleep, Little One, Sleep	PFE	N/A	N/A
Hum 457: Sound the Trumpet	1988	6-8	$75-$85
Hum 458: Storybook Time	1991	7-8	$280-$580
Hum 459: In the Meadow	1987	6-8	$150-$160
Hum 460: Tally dealer plaque	1986	6-7	$120-$900
Hum 461: In the Orchard	PFE	N/A	N/A
Hum 462: Tit for Tat	2004	8	$279
Hum 463: My Wish is Small	1985	6-7	$150-$1,500
Hum 464: Young Scholar	PFE	6	$2,400-$3,000
Hum 465: Where Shall I Go?	PFE	N/A	N/A
Hum 466: Do Re Mi	PFE	N/A	N/A

Hum 452: Flying High Christmas Ornament

Hum 453: The Accompanist

Hum 454: Song of Praise

Hum No./Name	Year	Trademarks	Value
Hum 467: The Kindergartner	1987	6-8	$70-$150
Hum 468: Come On	PFE	N/A	N/A
Hum 469: Starting Young	PFE	N/A	N/A
Hum 470: Time Out	2007	8	$299
Hum 471: Harmony in Four Parts	1989	6	$1,200-$1,500
Hum 472: On Our Way	1992	6-7	$720-$1,800
Hum 473: Ruprecht	1987	6-7	$300-$1,800
Hum 474: Gentle Care	PFE	N/A	N/A
Hum 475: Make a Wish	1989	6-7	$135-$150
Hum 476: A Winter Song	1988	6-8	$90-$145
Hum 477: A Budding Maestro	1988	6-7	$70-$85
Hum 478: I'm Here	1989	6-8	$85-$95
Hum 479: I Brought You a Gift	1989	6-7	$75-$110
Hum 480: Hosanna	1989	6-8	$80-$90

Hum 455: The Guardian

Hum 457: Sound the Trumpet

Hum 458: Storybook Time

Hum 459: In the Meadow

Hum No./Name	Year	Trademarks	Value
Hum 481: Love From Above Christmas ornament	1989	6	$75-$90
Hum 482: One For You, One For Me	1989	6-8	$55-$85
Hum 483: I'll Protect Him		6-8	$65-$75
Hum 484: Peace on Earth Christmas ornament	1990	6	$75-$80
Hum 485: A Gift From a Friend	1991	6-7	$150-$190
Hum 486: I Wonder	1990	6-7	$150-$190
Hum 487: Let's Tell the World	1990	6	$900-$1,080
Hum 488: What's That?	1997	7	$105-$115
Hum 489: Pretty Please	1996	7-8	$85-$135
Hum 490: Carefree	1997	7-8	$85-$135
Hum 491-492: Open Numbers			
Hum 493: Two Hands, One Treat	1991	7	$75-$90

Hum 460: Tally dealer plaque

Hum 462: Tit For Tat

Hum 463: My Wish is Small   Hum 467: The Kindergartner

Hum No./Name	Year	Trademarks	Value
Hum 494: Open Number			
Hum 495: Evening Prayer	1991	7-8	$80-$85
Hum 496-497: Open Numbers			
Hum 498: All Smiles	1997	7	$120-$135
Hum 499: Open Number			
Hum 500: Flowers For Mother	PFE	N/A	N/A
Hum 501-511: Doll Parts	N/A	N/A	N/A
Hum 512: Umbrella Girl Doll	N/A	N/A	$120-$150
Hum 513: Little Fiddler Doll	N/A	N/A	$120-$150
Hum 514: Friend or Foe? Doll	N/A	N/A	$120-$150
Hum 515: Kiss Me Doll	N/A	N/A	$120-$150
Hum 516: Merry Wanderer Doll	N/A	N/A	$120-$150
Hum 517: Goose Girl Doll	N/A	N/A	$120-$150
Hum 518: Umbrella Boy Doll	N/A	N/A	$120-$150

Hum 470: Time Out

Hum 471: Harmony in Four Parts

Hum 472: On Our Way

Hum 473: Ruprecht (Knecht Ruprecht)

Hum 475: Make a Wish

Hum 476: A Winter Song

Hum 477: A Budding Maestro

Hum 478: I'm Here

Hum 479: I Brought You a Gift

Hum 480: Hosanna

Hum 481: Love From Above
1989 Christmas ornament

Hum No./Name	Year	Trademarks	Value
Hum 519: Ride Into Christmas Doll	N/A	N/A	$120-$150
Hum 520: PFE	N/A	N/A	N/A
Hum 521: School Girl Doll	N/A	N/A	$120-$150
Hum 522: Little Scholar Doll	N/A	N/A	$120-$150
Hum 523: PFE	N/A	N/A	N/A
Hum 524: Valentine Gift Doll	N/A	N/A	$120-$150
Hum 525-529: Open Numbers			
Hum 530: Land in Sight	1991	7	$1,080-$1,350
Hum 531-532: Open Numbers			
Hum 533: Ooh, My Tooth	1995	7-8	$90-$95
Hum 534: A Nap	1991	6-8	$85-$150
Hum 535: No Thank You	1996	7-8	$80-$85
Hum 536: Christmas Surprise	1998	7-8	$50-$120
Hum 537: Open Number			

Hum 482: One For You, One For Me

Hum 484: Peace On Earth 1990 Christmas ornament

Hum 485: A Gift From a Friend

Hum 486: I Wonder

Hum 487: Let's Tell the World

Hum 488: What's That?

Hum 489: Pretty Please

Hum 490: Carefree

Hum 493: Two Hands, One Treat

Hum No./Name	Year	Trademarks	Value
Hum 538: School's Out	1997	7-8	$115-$120
Hum 539: Good News	1996	7-8	$125-$135
Hum 540: Best Wishes	1996	7-8	$120-$200
Hum 541: Sweet As Can Be	1993	7-8	$105-$149
Hum 542: Open Number			
Hum 543: I'm Sorry	PFE	N/A	N/A
Hum 544: Open Number			
Hum 545: Come Back Soon	1995	6-8	$110-$300
Hum 546: Open Number			
Hum 547: Bunny's Mother	2006	8	$109
Hum 548: Flower Girl	1990	6-8	$105-$175
Hum 549: A Sweet Offering	1993	7	$90-$95
Hum 550-552: Open Numbers			
Hum 553: Scamp	1992	7-8	$90-$135
Hum 554: Cheeky Fellow	1992	7-8	$90-$135
Hum 555: One, Two, Three	1996	7	$90-$150
Hum 556: One Plus One	1993	7-8	$105-$120
Hum 557: Strum Along	1995	7-8	$105-$155
Hum 558: Little Troubadour	1994	7-8	$90-$145
Hum 559: Heart and Soul	1996	7-8	$90-$135
Hum 560: Lucky Fellow	1992	7	$60-$90
Hum 561: Grandma's Girl	1990	6-8	$110-$180
Hum 562: Grandpa's Boy	1990	6-8	$110-$180
Hum 563: Little Visitor	1994	7	$120-$125
Hum 564: Free Spirit	1996	7-8	$90-$135
Hum 565: Open Number			
Hum 566: The Angler	1995	7-8	$240-$245
Hum 567-568: Open Numbers			
Hum 569: A Free Flight	1993	7-8	$125-$145
Hum 570: Open Number			
Hum 571: Angelic Guide Christmas ornament	1991	6-7	$85-$120

Hum 495: Evening Prayer

Hum 498: All Smiles

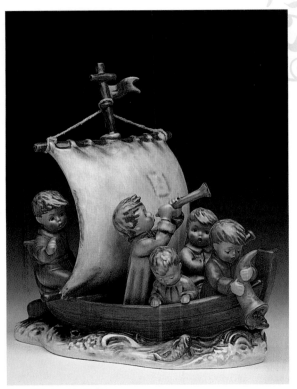

Hum 530: Land in Sight

Hum 533: Ooh, My Tooth

Hum 534: A Nap

Hum 535: No Thank You

Hum 536: Christmas Surprise

Hum 538: School's Out

Hum 539: Good News   Hum 540: Best Wishes

Hum No./Name	Year	Trademarks	Value
Hum 572: Country Devotion	PFE	N/A	N/A
Hum 573: Loving Wishes/ Will You Be Mine?	2004	8	$219
Hum 574: Rock-A-Bye	1994	7	$840-$960
HUM 575-582, 585, 586: ANGELS OF CHRISTMAS ORNAMENT SERIES			
	1990	6-7	$40-$50 ea.
Hum 575: Heavenly Angel			
Hum 576: Festival Harmony With Mandolin			
Hum 577: Festival Harmony With Flute			
Hum 578: Celestial Musician			
Hum 579: Song of Praise			
Hum 580: Angel With Lute			
Hum 581: Prayer of Thanks			
Hum 582: Gentle Song			
Hum 585: Angel in Cloud			
Hum 586: Angel With Trumpet			

Hum 541: Sweet As Can Be

Hum 545: Come Back Soon

Hum 548: Flower Girl

Hum 549: A Sweet Offering

Hum 553: Scamp

Hum 554: Cheeky Fellow

Hum 555: One, Two, Three

Hum 556: One Plus One

Hum 557: Strum Along

Hum 559: Heart and Soul

Hum 560: Lucky Fellow

Hum 561: Grandma's Girl

Hum 562: Grandpa's Boy

Hum 563: Little Visitor

Hum 564: Free Spirit

Hum 566: The Angler

Hum 569: A Free Flight

Hum 571: Angelic Guide 1991 Christmas ornament

Hum 573: Will You Be Mine?   Hum 574: Rock-A-Bye

Hum No./Name	Year	Trademarks	Value
Hum 583-584, 587-595: Open Numbers			
Hum 596: Thanksgiving Prayer Christmas ornament	1997	7	$80-$85
Hum 597: Echoes of Joy Christmas ornament	1998	7	$80-$85
Hum 598: Joyful Noise Christmas ornament	1999	7	$80-$85
Hum 599: Light the Way Christmas ornament	1997	7	$80-$85
Hum 600: We Wish You the Best	1991	6-7	$1,050-$1,260
Hum 601-607: Open Numbers			
Hum 608: Blossom Time	1996	7-8	$105-$130
Hum IV/608: Blossom Time	1999	7	$180-$240
Hum 609: Open Number			
Hum 610: April Showers	2005	8	$450

Hum 596: Thanksgiving Prayer ornament

Hum 597: Echoes of Joy ornament

Hum 598: Joyful Noise ornament

Hum 599: Light the Way ornament

Hum 600: We Wish You the Best

Hum 608: Blossom Time

Hum No./Name	Year	Trademarks	Value
Hum 611: Sunny Song	PFE	N/A	N/A
Hum 612: Lazybones	2004	8	$259
Hum 613: What's Up?	PFE	N/A	N/A
Hum 614: Harmonica Player	PFE	N/A	N/A
Hum 615: Private Conversation	1990	7	$160-$200
Hum 616: Parade of Lights	1993	7-8	$210-$285
Hum 617: Open Number			
Hum 618: A Basket of Gifts	2002	8	$375
Hum 619: Garden Gift	2003	8	$279
Hum 620: A Story From Grandma	1995	7	$900-$1,600
Hum 621: At Grandpa's	1994	7	$900-$1,600
Hum 622: Light Up the Night Christmas ornament	1992	7	$90-$150

Hum No./Name	Year	Trademarks	Value
Hum 623: Herald on High Christmas ornament	1993	7	$90-$150
Hum 624: Fresh Blossoms	2006	8	$199
Hum 625: Goose Girl vase	1997	7	$50-$75
Hum 626: I Didn't Do It	1993	7	$150-$225
Hum 627: Open Number			
Hum 628: Gentle Fellowship	1995	7	$360-$500
Hum 629: From Me to You	1995	7	$80-$125
Hum 630: For Keeps	1994	7	$80-$125
Hum 631: Open Number			
Hum 632: At Play	1998	7	$170-$200
Hum 633: I'm Carefree	1994	7-8	$265-$600
Hum 634: Sunshower	1997	7-8	$280-$359
Hum 635: Welcome Spring	1993	7	$960-$1,100
Hum 636-637: Open Numbers			
Hum 638: The Botanist vase	1998	7	$50-$75
Hum 639-640: Open Numbers			
Hum 641: Thanksgiving Prayer	1997	7-8	$80-$180
Hum 642: Echoes of Joy	1997	7-8	$80-$180
Hum 643: Joyful Noise	1999	7-8	$80-$180
Hum 644: Open Number			
Hum 645: Christmas Song annual ornament	1996	7	$80-$120
Hum 646: Celestial Musician annual ornament	1993	7	$80-$100
Hum 647: Festival Harmony With Mandolin annual ornament	1994	7	$80-$100
Hum 648: Festival Harmony With Flute annual ornament	1995	7	$80-$100
Hum 649: Fascination	1996	7	$120-$190
Hum 650-657: Open Numbers			

Hum 610: April Showers

Hum 615: Private Conversation

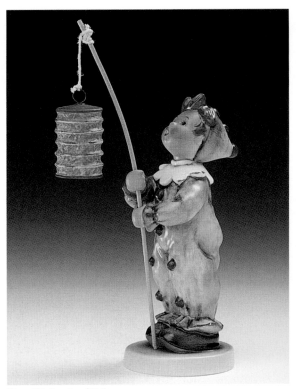

Hum 616: Parade of Lights

Hum 618: A Basket of Gifts

Hum 619: Garden Gift

Hum 620: A Story From Grandma

Hum 621: At Grandpa's

Hum 622: Light Up the Night 1992 Christmas ornament

Hum 623: Herald on High 1993 Christmas ornament

Hum 624: Fresh Blossoms

Hum 625: Goose Girl vase

Hum 626: I Didn't Do It

Hum 628: Gentle Fellowship

Hum 629: From Me to You

Hum 630: For Keeps

Hum 632: At Play

Hum 633: I'm Carefree

Hum 634: Sunshower

Hum 635: Welcome Spring

Hum 641: Thanksgiving Prayer

Hum 642: Echoes of Joy   Hum 643: Joyful Noise

Hum No./Name	Year	Trademarks	Value
Hum 658: Playful Blessing	1997	7	$170-$260
Hum 659: Open Number			
Hum 660: Fond Goodbye	1997	7	$960-$1,450
Hum 661: My Little Lamb	2005	8	$119
Hum 662: Friends Together	1993	7-8	$210-$475
Hum 663-666: Open Numbers			
Hum 667: Pretty as a Picture	PFE	N/A	N/A
Hum 668: Strike Up the Band	1995	7	$840-$1,200
Hum 669-674: Kitchen Moulds	1991	6-7	$99-$115 ea.
Hum 675: Open Number			
Hum 676, 677: Apple Tree Girl and Apple Tree Boy candleholders	1989	6-7	$120-$150
Hum 678, 679: She Loves Me, She Loves Me Not and Good Friends candleholders	1990	6-7	$120-$150

Hum 645: Christmas Song annual ornament

Hum 646: Celestial Musician 1993 annual ornament

Hum 647: Festival Harmony With Mandolin annual ornament

Hum 648: Festival Harmony With Flute annual ornament

Hum 649: Fascination

Hum No./Name	Year	Trademarks	Value
Hum 680-683: Open Numbers			
Hum 684: Thoughtful trinket box	2002	8	$25-$40
Hum 685: Book Worm trinket box	2002	8	$25-$40
Hum 686: Sweet Greetings trinket box	2002	8	$25-$40
Hum 687: She Loves Me, She Loves Me Not trinket box	2002	8	$25-$40
Hum 688: Umbrella Boy trinket box	2002	8	$25-$40
Hum 689: Umbrella Girl trinket box	2002	8	$25-$40
Hum 690: Smiling Through plaque	1978	5	$25-$40
Hum 691: Open Number			
Hum 692: Christmas Song annual Christmas plate	1996	7	$25-$40
Hum 693: Festival Harmony With Flute annual Christmas plate	1995	7	$25-$40
Hum 694: Thanksgiving Prayer annual Christmas plate	1997	7	$25-$40
Hum 695: Echoes of Joy annual Christmas plate	1998	7	$25-$60
Hum 696: Joyful Noise annual Christmas plate	1999	7	$25-$60
Hum 697: Light the Way annual Christmas plate	2000	7	$25-$60
Hum 698: Heart's Delight	1998	7-8	$150-$220
Hum 699: Love in Bloom	1997	7-8	$150-$220
HUM 700-714: ANNUAL BELLS			
Hum 700: Let's Sing	1978	5	$25-$50
Hum 701: Farewell	1979	5	$20-$30
Hum 702: Thoughtful	1980	6	$25-$30
Hum 703: In Tune	1981	6	$25-$50
Hum 704: She Loves Me, She Loves Me Not	1982	6	$30-$40

Hum 658: Playful Blessing

Hum No./Name	Year	Trademarks	Value
Hum 705: Knit One, Purl One	1983	6	$30-$40
Hum 706: Mountaineer	1984	6	$30-$40
Hum 707: Girl With Sheet Music	1985	6	$30-$40
Hum 708: Sing Along	1986	6	$40-$75
Hum 709: With Loving Greetings	1987	6	$40-$75
Hum 710: Busy Student	1988	6	$40-$75
Hum 711: Latest News	1989	6	$40-$75

Hum 660: Fond Goodbye

Hum 661: My Little Lamb

Hum 662: Friends Together

Hum 668: Strike Up the Band

Hum 690: Smiling Through wall plaque

Hum 698: Heart's Delight

Hum 699: Love In Bloom

Hummel® Listings

Hum No./Name	Year	Trademarks	Value
Hum 712: What's New	1990	6	$40-$75
Hum 713: Favorite Pet	1991	6	$40-$75
Hum 714: Whistler's Duet	1992	6	$40-$75
Hum 715: Light the Way	1999	8	$95-$180
Hum 716: Open Number			
Hum 717: Valentine Gift display plaque	1996	7	$180-$250
Hum 718: Heavenly Angels (5)	1999	7	$60-$90 ea.
Hum 719: Open Number			
Hum 720: On Parade	1998	7-8	$165-$180
Hum 721: Trio of Wishes	1997	7	$360-$475
Hum 722: Little Visitor plaque	1995	7-8	$95-$120
Hum 723: Silent Vigil	PFE	N/A	N/A
Hum 724-725: Open Numbers			
Hum 726: Soldier Boy plaque	1996	7	$120-$140
Hum 727: Garden Treasures	1998	7	$90-$100
Hum 728: Open Number			
Hum 729: Nature's Gift	1997	7	$90-$100
Hum 730: Just Resting bell	1985	6	$900-$1,200
Hum 731: Best Friends	2005	8	$399
Hum 732: For My Sweetheart	PFE	N/A	N/A
Hum 733-734: Open Numbers			
HUM 735-738: CELEBRATION PLATE SERIES			
Hum 735: It's Cold	1989	N/A	$50-$60
Hum 736: Daisies Don't Tell	1988	N/A	$50-$60
Hum 737: Valentine's Joy	1987	N/A	$50-$60
Hum 738: Valentine Gift	1986	N/A	$50-$60
Hum 739/I: Call to Glory	1994	7-8	$250-$295
Hum 740: Open Number			
HUM 741-744: LITTLE MUSIC MAKERS MINI PLATE SERIES			
Hum 741: Serenade	1985	N/A	$25-$30

Hum 715: Light the Way

Hum 717: Valentine Gift plaque

Hum No./Name	Year	Trademarks	Value
Hum 742: Band Leader	1987	N/A	$25-$30
Hum 743: Soloist	1986	N/A	$25-$30
Hum 744: Little Fiddler	1984	N/A	$25-$30
HUM 745-748: LITTLE HOMEMAKERS MINI PLATE SERIES			
Hum 745: Little Sweeper	1988	N/A	$25-$30
Hum 746: Wash Day	1989	N/A	$25-$30

Hum 720: On Parade

Hum 721: Trio of Wishes

Hum 727: Garden Treasures

Hum 729: Nature's Gift

Hum No./Name	Year	Trademarks	Value
Hum 747: A Stitch in Time	1990	N/A	$25-$30
Hum 748: Chicken-Licken	1991	N/A	$25-$30
Hum 749: Open Number			
Hum 750: Goose Girl anniversary clock	1995	7-8	$200-$250
Hum 751: Love's Bounty	1996	7	$1,100-$1,200
Hum 752: Open Number			
Hum 753: Togetherness	2006	8	$745
Hum 754: We Come in Peace	1994	7	$240-$350
Hum 755: Heavenly Angel tree topper	1994	7	$450-$500
Hum 756: The Artist display plaque	1993	7	$240-$300
Hum 757: Tuneful Trio	1996	7	$450-$500
Hum 758: Nimble Fingers	1996	7-8	$225-$250
Hum 759: To Keep You Warm	1995	7-8	$195-$260
Hum 760: Country Suitor	1995	7	$195-$225
Hum 761: From the Heart	1996	7-8	$120-$135
Hum 762: Roses Are Red	1997	7-8	$120-$135
Hum 763: Happy Returns	PFE	N/A	N/A
Hum 764: Mission Madonna	PFE	N/A	N/A
Hum 765: First Love	2004	8	$945
Hum 766: Here's My Heart	1998	7	$960-$1,375
Hum 767: Puppy Love display plaque	1995	7	$180-$240
Hum 768: Pixie	1995	7-8	$105-$140
Hum 769-770: Open Numbers			
Hum 771: Practice Makes Perfect (boy)	1997	7-8	$139-$280
Hum 772-774: Open Numbers			
HUM 775-786: CHRISTMAS BELLS			
Hum 775: Ride Into Christmas	1989	6	$30-$40

Hum 731: Best Friends

Hum 739/I: Call to Glory

Hum 751: Love's Bounty

Hum 753: Togetherness

Hum 754: We Come in Peace

Hum No./Name	Year	Trademarks	Value
Hum 776: Letter to Santa Claus	1990	6	$30-$40
Hum 777: Hear Ye, Hear Ye	1991	7	$30-$40
Hum 778: Harmony in Four Parts	1992	7	$30-$40
Hum 779: Celestial Musician	1993	7	$25-$35
Hum 780: Festival Harmony With Mandolin	1994	7	$25-$35
Hum 781: Festival Harmony With Flute	1995	7	$25-$35
Hum 782: Christmas Song	1996	7	$25-$35
Hum 783: Thanksgiving Prayer	1997	7	$70-$75

Hum 755: Heavenly Angel tree topper

Hum 757: Tuneful Trio

Hum 758: Nimble Fingers

Hum No./Name	Year	Trademarks	Value
Hum 784: Echoes of Joy	1998	7	$70-$75
Hum 785: Joyful Noise	1999	7	$70-$75
Hum 786: Light the Way	2000	8	$70-$75
Hum 787: Traveling Trio	1997	7	$490-$500
Hum 788/A: Hello and Hum 788/B: Sister perpetual calendars	1995	7	$100-$180 ea.
Hum 789: Open Number			
Hum 790: Celebrate With Song	1996	7	$180-$250

Hum 759: To Keep You Warm

Hum 760: Country Suitor

Hum 761: From the Heart

Hum 762: Roses Are Red

Hum 765: First Love

Hum No./Name	Year	Trademarks	Value
Hum 791: May Dance	2000	8	$130-$199
Hum 792: Open Number			
Hum 793: Forever Yours	1996	7	$55-$100
Hum 794: Best Buddies	PFE	N/A	N/A
Hum 795: From My Garden	1997	7-9	$180-$220
Hum 796: Brave Voyager	1994	8	$499
Hum 797: Rainy Day Bouquet	PFE	N/A	N/A
Hum 798: Open Number			
Hum 799: Vagabond	PFE	N/A	N/A
Hum 800: Proud Moments	1999	8	$279
Hum 801: Open Number			
Hum 802: Brave Soldier	1997	8	$228

Hum 766: Here's My Heart

Hum 767: Puppy Love 60-year anniversary display plaque

Hum No./Name	Year	Trademarks	Value
Hum 803: Little Fisherman	2003	8	$70
Hum 804: Love Petals	2003	8	$70
Hum 805: Little Toddler	PFE	N/A	N/A
Hum 806-813, 824-825, 831-832, 834, 841-842, 851-854, 904, 913, 947 and 968: International Figurines			
806: Bulgarian Boy	N/A	N/A	$10-$15,000
807: Bulgarian Girl	N/A	N/A	$10-$15,000
808: Bulgarian Boy	N/A	N/A	$10-$15,000
809: Bulgarian Girl	N/A	N/A	$10-$15,000
810(A): Bulgarian Girl	N/A	N/A	$10-$15,000
810(B): Bulgarian Girl	N/A	N/A	$10-$15,000

Hum 768: Pixie

Hum 771: Practice Makes Perfect

Hum 787: Traveling Trio

Hum 790: Celebrate With Song   Hum 791: May Dance

Hum No./Name	Year	Trademarks	Value
811: Bulgarian Boy	N/A	N/A	$10-$15,000
812(A): Serbian Girl	N/A	N/A	$10-$15,000
812(B): Serbian Girl	N/A	N/A	$10-$15,000
813: Serbian Boy	N/A	N/A	$10-$15,000
824(A): Swedish Boy	N/A	N/A	$10-$15,000
824(B): Swedish Boy	N/A	N/A	$10-$15,000
825(A): Swedish Girl	N/A	N/A	$10-$15,000
825(B): Swedish Girl	N/A	N/A	$10-$15,000
831: Slovak Boy	N/A	N/A	$10-$15,000
832(B): Slovak Girl	N/A	N/A	$10-$15,000
832: Slovak Boy	N/A	N/A	$10-$15,000

Hum 793: Forever Yours

Hum 795: From My Garden

Hum 800: Proud Moments

Hum 802: Brave Soldier

Hummel® Listings

Hum No./Name	Year	Trademarks	Value
834: Slovak Boy	N/A	N/A	$10-$15,000
841: Czech Boy	N/A	N/A	$10-$15,000
842(A): Czech Girl	N/A	N/A	$10-$15,000
842(B): Czech Girl	N/A	N/A	$10-$15,000
851: Hungarian Boy	N/A	N/A	$10-$15,000
852(A): Hungarian Girl	N/A	N/A	$10-$15,000
852(B): Hungarian Girl	N/A	N/A	$10-$15,000
853(A): Hungarian Boy	N/A	N/A	$10-$15,000
853(B): Hungarian Boy	N/A	N/A	$10-$15,000
854: Hungarian Girl	N/A	N/A	$10-$15,000
904: Serbian Boy	N/A	N/A	$10-$15,000
913: Serbian Girl	N/A	N/A	$10-$15,000
947: Serbian Girl	N/A	N/A	$10-$15,000
968: Serbian Boy	N/A	N/A	$10-$15,000
Hum 814: Peaceful Blessing	1998	7-8	$180-$200
Hum 815: Heavenly Prayer	1998	7-8	$180-$200
Hum 816-819: Open Numbers			
Hum 820: Adieu plaque	1999	7	$95-$125
Hum 822: Hummelnest plaque	1997	7-8	$125
Hum 823: Open Number			
Hum 824-825: Swedish figurines (see Hum 806: International Figurines)			
Hum 826: Little Maestro	2000	8	$320-$350
Hum 827: Daydreamer plaque	1999	7-8	$140
Hum 828: Over the Horizon plaque	2000	8	$140
Hum 829: Where to Go?	1999	7	$358
Hum 830: Open Number			
Hum 831-834: Slovak figurines (see Hum 806: International Figurines)			
Hum 835: Garden Splendor	2000	8	$219
Hum 836: Afternoon Nap	2001	8	$225
Hum 837: Bumblebee Friend	2002	8	$279
Hum 838: Christmas By Candlelight	2001	8	$215

Hum 803: Little Fisherman

Hum 804: Love Petals

Hum 814: Peaceful Blessing

Hum 815: Heavenly Prayer

Hummel® Listings

Hum No./Name	Year	Trademarks	Value
Hum 839-844: Open Numbers			
Hum 841-842: Czech figurines (see Hum 806: International Figurines)			
Hum 845: Too Shy to Sing	2003	8	$90
Hum 846: Hitting the High Note	2004	8	$110
Hum 847: Lamplight Caroler	2006	8	$110
Hum 848: Steadfast Soprano	2005	8	$100
Hum 849: Double Delight	2009	8	$269
Hum 850: Open Number			
Hum 851-854: Hungarian figurines (see Hum 806: International Figurines)			
Hum 855: Millennium Madonna	2000	7	$495-$550
Hum 856: A Heartfelt Gift	2003	8	$275
Hum 857: Accordion Ballad	2004	8	$70
Hum 858/A: A Favorite Pet Easter egg	2001	8	$56
Hum 859: Open Number			
HUM 860-874: MINIATURE BELLS			
Hum 860: Let's Sing	N/A	8	$25
Hum 861: Farewell	N/A	8	$25
Hum 862: Thoughtful	N/A	8	$25
Hum 863: In Tune	N/A	8	$25
Hum 864: She Loves Me, She Loves Me Not	N/A	8	$25
Hum 865: Knit One, Purl One	N/A	8	$25
Hum 866: Mountaineer	N/A	8	$25
Hum 867: Girl With Sheet Music	N/A	8	$25
Hum 868: Sing Along	N/A	8	$25
Hum 869: With Loving Greetings	N/A	8	$25
Hum 870: Busy Student	N/A	8	$25
Hum 871: Latest News	N/A	8	$25
Hum 872: What's New?	N/A	8	$25
Hum 873: Favorite Pet	N/A	8	$25

Hum 826: Little Maestro

Hum 835: Garden Splendor

Hum 836: Afternoon Nap

Hum 837: Bumblebee Friend

Hum 838: Christmas By Candlelight

Hum 845: Too Shy to Sing

Hum 846: Hitting the High Note

Hum 847: Lamplight Caroler

Hum 848: Steadfast Soprano

Hum No./Name	Year	Trademarks	Value
Hum 874: Whistler's Duet	N/A	8	$25
Hum 875: Open Number			
Hum 876/A: Heavenly Angel ornament	1999	7	$20
Hum 877/A: Ride Into Christmas ornament	1999	7	$10
Hum 878/A: Sleep Tight ornament	1999	7	$10
Hum 879/A: Christmas Song ornament	2002	8	$10
Hum 880/A: Hear Ye, Hear Ye ornament	2002	8	$10
Hum 881-884: New Baby Gifts	2003	8	$22.50-$75
Hum 885: Fishing Adventure	2004	8	$250
HUM 886-899: CENTURY COLLECTION MINI PLATES			
Hum 886: Chapel Time	1986	N/A	$30

Hum 849: Double Delight

Hum 855: Millennium Madonna

Hum 856: A Heartfelt Gift

Hum 885: Fishing Adventure   Hum 902: Sunflowers, My Love?

Hum No./Name	Year	Trademarks	Value
Hum 887: Pleasant Journey	1987	N/A	$30
Hum 888: Call to Worship	1988	N/A	$30
Hum 889: Harmony In Four Parts	1989	N/A	$30
Hum 890: Let's Tell the World	1990	N/A	$30
Hum 891: We Wish You the Best	1991	N/A	$30
Hum 892: On Our Way	1992	N/A	$30
Hum 893: Welcome Spring	1993	N/A	$30
Hum 894: Rock-A-Bye	1994	N/A	$30
Hum 895: Strike Up the Band	1995	N/A	$30
Hum 896: Love's Bounty	1996	N/A	$30
Hum 897: Fond Goodbye	1997	N/A	$30
Hum 898: Here's My Heart	1998	N/A	$30
Hum 899: Fanfare	1999	N/A	$30

Hum 903: Adoring Children

Hum 905: Come With Me

Hum 906: I Will Follow You

Hum 907: Big Fish

Hum 908: Gone A-Wandering

Hum 909: Gifts of Love

Hum 911: Harmony & Lyric

Hum No./Name	Year	Trademarks	Value
Hum 900: Merry Wanderer plaque	1999	8	$120
Hum 901: Open Number			
Hum 902: Sunflowers, My Love?	2004	8	$275
Hum 903: Adoring Children	2006	8	$259
Hum 904: Serbian Boy (see Hum 806: International Figurines)			
Hum 905: Come With Me	2006	8	$99
Hum 906: I Will Follow You	2007	8	$109
Hum 907: Big Fish	N/A	8	$99
Hum 908: Gone A-Wandering	2006	8	$199
Hum 909: Gifts of Love	2006	8	$350
Hum 911: Harmony & Lyric	N/A	8	$350
Hum 912/A through 912/D: Spring Time, Spring Waltz, Spring Love, and Spring Fancy	2007	8	$125 ea.

Hum 912/A, B, C, D:
Spring Time, Spring Waltz, Spring Love, Spring Fancy

Hum No./Name	Year	Trademarks	Value
Hum 913: Serbian Girl (see Hum 806: International Figurines)			
Hum 914: Blumenkinder	2008	8	$269
Hum 915: Tuning Up	2008	8	$449
Hum 920: Star Gazer annual plate	2000	8	$125-$198
Hum 921: Garden Splendor annual plate	2000	8	$125-$198
Hum 922: Afternoon Nap annual plate	2001	8	$125-$198
Hum 923: Bumblebee Friend annual plate	2002	8	$125-$198
Hum 924: The Florist annual plate	2003	8	$125-$200
Hum 925: Garden Gift annual plate	2004	8	$125-$200
Hum 926-946: Open Numbers			
Hum 947: Serbian Girl (see Hum 806: International Figurines)			
Hum 948-949: Open Numbers			
Hum 950: Apple Tree Girl doll	1998	7	$100-$250
Hum 951: Apple Tree Boy doll	1998	7	$100-$250
Hum 952-959: Open Numbers			
Hum 960: Ride Into Christmas doll	1999	7	$100-$200
Hum 961-967: Open Numbers			
Hum 968: Serbian Boy (see Hum 806: International Figurines)			
Hum 969: Puppy Love clock	2005	8	$250
Hum 970: In Tune clock	2005	8	$250
Hum 971-995: M.I. Hummel miniature plate series	1997-98	7	N/A
Hum 996: Scamp trinket box	2002	8	$20-$40
Hum 997: Pixie trinket box	2002	8	$20-$40
Hum 998-1998: Open Numbers			
Hum 1999: Fanfare	1999	7	$1,200-$1,300
Hum 2000: Worldwide Wanderers	1999	8	$4,500

Hum 915: Tuning Up

Hum 920: Star Gazer annual plate

Hum 1999: Fanfare

Hum 2000: Worldwide Wanderers

Hum No./Name	Year	Trademarks	Value
Hum 2001: Christmas is Coming	2009	9	$459
Hum 2002: Making New Friends	1996	7-8	$595-$625
Hum 2003: Dearly Beloved	1998	708	$219-$450
Hum 2004: Pretzel Girl	1999	7	$185-$200
Hum 2005-2006: Open Numbers			
Hum 2007: Tender Love	1998	7	$198
Hum 2008: Frisky Friends	1997	7	$198
Hum 2009: Sleepy Doll	2007	8	$199
Hum 2010: Open Number			
Hum 2011: Little Landscaper	2002	8	$200-$259
Hum 2012: Saint Nicholas Day	1997	7	$250-$450
Hum 2013: Surprise Visit	2002	8	$219
Hum 2014: Christmas Delivery	1997	7-8	$279-$1,550

Hum 2001: Christmas is Coming

Hum No./Name	Year	Trademarks	Value
Hum 2015: Wonder of Christmas	1998	7-8	$400-$500
Hum 2016: Tasty Treats	2009	9	$529
Hum 2017: Open Number			
Hum 2018: Toyland Express	2002	8	$219
Hum 2019: My Favorite Pony	2002	8	$150-$219
Hum 2020: Riding Lesson	2001	8	$150-$219
Hum 2021: Cowboy Corral	2001	8	$150-$219
Hum 2022-2024: Open Numbers			
Hum 2025/A: Wishes Come True	2000	8	$250-$695

Hum 2002: Making New Friends

Hum 2003: Dearly Beloved

Hum 2004: Pretzel Girl

Hum 2007: Tender Love

Hum 2008: Frisky Friends

Hum 2009: Sleepy Doll

Hum 2011: Little Landscaper

Hum 2012: Saint Nicholas Day

Hum 2013: Surprise Visit

Hum No./Name	Year	Trademarks	Value
Hum 2026: Good Tidings	2003	8	$199
Hum 2027: Easter's Coming	2001	8	$179-$240
Hum 2028: Winter Adventure	2001	8	$139-$230
Hum 2029: Open Number			
Hum 2030: Firefighter	1999	8	$180-$250
Hum 2031: Catch of the Day	2000	8	$175-$205

Hum 2014: Christmas Delivery

Hum 2015: Wonder of Christmas Collector's Set with Steiff bear

Hum 2016: Tasty Treats

Hum 2018: Toyland Express

Hum 2019: My Favorite Pony

Hum 2020: Riding Lesson

Hum 2021: Cowboy Corral

Hum 2025/A: Wishes Come True

Hum 2026: Good Tidings

Hum 2027: Easter's Coming

Hum 2028: Winter Adventure

Hum 2030: Firefighter

Hum 2031: Catch of the Day

Hum No./Name	Year	Trademarks	Value
Hum 2032: Puppy Pause	2001	8	$150-$219
Hum 2033: Kitty Kisses	2001	8	$150-$219
Hum 2034: Good Luck Charm	2001	8	$110-$179
Hum 2035: First Snow	1999	7-8	$149-$370
Hum 2036: Let It Snow	1999	7-8	$139-$280
Hum 2037: Star Light, Star Bright	2005	8	$275-$305
Hum 2038: In the Kitchen	1999	7-8	$150-$200
Hum 2039: Halt!	2000	8	$150-$200
Hum 2040: One Coat or Two?	2000	8	$150-$200
Hum 2041-2042: Open Numbers			
Hum 2043/A: Just Horsin' Around	2007	8	$189
Hum 2043/B: Pony Express	2007	8	$189
Hum 2044: All Aboard	1997	8	$205-$210
Hum 2045: Trail Blazer	2006	8	$249
Hum 2046: Open Number			

Hum 2032: Puppy Pause

Hum 2033: Kitty Kisses

Hum No./Name	Year	Trademarks	Value
Hum 2047: Winter Sleigh Ride	2002	8	$225
Hum 2048: Little Patriot	2002	8	$450-$550
Hum 2049/A: Cuddles	1998	7-8	$70-$75
Hum 2049/B: My Best Friend	1998	7-8	$70-$75
Hum 2050/A: Messages of Love	1999	7-8	$70-$75
Hum 2050/B: Be Mine	1999	7-8	$70-$75
Hum 2051/A: Once Upon a Time	1998	7-8	$70-$75
Hum 2051/B: Let's Play	1998	7-8	$70-$75
Hum 2052: Pigtails	1999	7	$70-$80
Hum 2053: Playful Pals	1998	7	$110-$150
Hum 2054-2057: Open Numbers			
Hum 2058/A: Skating Lesson	2000	8	$110-$150
Hum 2058/B: Skate in Stride	2000	8	$110-$155
Hum 2059: Merry Wandress	2004	8	$125-$180
Hum 2060: European Wanderer	1999	8	$100-$200

Hum 2034: Good Luck Charm

Hum 2035: First Snow

Hum 2036: Let It Snow

Hum 2037: Star Light, Star Bright

Hum 2038: In the Kitchen   Hum 2039: Halt!

Hum No./Name	Year	Trademarks	Value
Hum 2061: American Wanderer	1999	8	$100-$200
Hum 2062: African Wanderer	1999	8	$100-$200
Hum 2063: Asian Wanderer	1999	8	$100-$200
Hum 2064: Australian Wanderer	1999	8	$100-$200
Hum 2065: Open Number			
Hum 2066: Peaceful Offering	1999	7	$100-$200
Hum 2067/A: Sweet Treats	2000	7-8	$70-$75
Hum 2067/B: For Me?	2000	8	$70-$75
Hum 2068/A: Bumblebee Blossom	2003	8	$70-$75
Hum 2068/B: A Four-Leaf Clover/ Pledge to America	2003/ 2004	8	$70-$75
Hum 2069/A: Monkey Business/ Freedom Day	2003/ 2005	8	$70-$75
Hum 2070: Scooter Time	2001	8	$500-$695
Hum 2071: Lucky Charmer	1999	7	$70-$75

Hum 2040: One Coat or Two?

Hum 2043/A: Just Horsin' Around

Hum 2043/B: Pony Express

Hum 2044: All Aboard

Hum 2045: Trail Blazer

Hum 2048: Little Patriot

Hum 2049/A: Cuddles

Hum 2049/B: My Best Friend

Hum 2050/A: Messages of Love

Hum 2050/B: Be Mine

Hum 2051/A: Once Upon a Time

Hum 2051/B: Let's Play

Hum 2052: Pigtails

Hum 2053: Playful Pals

Hum No./Name	Year	Trademarks	Value
Hum 2072: Winter Days	2004	8	$359-$500
Hum 2073/A: Ring in the Season	2001	8	$95-$139
Hum 2073/B: Christmas Carol	2001	8	$95-$139
Hum 2074/A: Christmas Gift	1998, 1999	7-8	$80-$95
Hum 2075: Comfort and Care	2000	8	$175-$255
Hum 2076: Open Number			
Hum 2077/A: First Bloom	1999	8	$70-$75
Hum 2077/B: A Flower For You	2000	8	$70-$75
Hum 2078: My Toy Train	2003	8	$70
Hum 2079/A: All By Myself	2003	8	$100-$140

Hum 2058/A: Skating Lesson

Hum 2058/B: Skate In Stride

Hum 2066: Peaceful Offering

Hum 2067/A: Sweet Treats

Hum 2067/B: For Me?

Hum 2068/A: Bumblebee Blossom

Hum 2068/B: A Four-Leaf Clover/Pledge to America

Hum 2069/A: Monkey Business/Freedom Day

Hum 2070: Scooter Time

Hum 2071: Lucky Charmer

Hum 2072: Winter Days

Hum 2073/A: Ring in the Season

Hum 2073/B: Christmas Carol

Hum 2074/A: Christmas Gift

Hum 2075: Comfort and Care

Hum 2077/A: First Bloom

Hum 2077/B: A Flower for You

Hum 2078: My Toy Train

Hum 2079/A: All By Myself

Hum No./Name	Year	Trademarks	Value
Hum 2079/B: Windy Wishes	2003	8	$100-$140
Hum 2080/A: Sharing a Story	2010	9	$299
Hum 2080/B: Here I Come	2010	9	$169
Hum 2081: Open Number			
Hum 2082: Oh, No!	2008	8	$399
Hum 2083: Open Number			
Hum 2084/A: Jump for Joy	2004	8	$195-$305
Hum 2084/B: Count Me In	2004	8	$195-$305
Hum 2085: Little Farm Hand	1999	8	$195-$225
Hum 2086: Spring Sowing	2000	8	$195-$225
Hum 2087/A: Sharpest Student	2000	8	$50-$95
Hum 2087/B: Honor Student	2000	8	$50-$95
Hum 2088/A: Playing Around	2003	8	$140-$200
Hum 2088/B: Rolling Around	2002	8	$140-$200
Hum 2089/A: Looking Around	2001	8	$150-$230
Hum 2089/B: Waiting Around	2004	8	$150-$230
Hum 2090: Open Number			
Hum 2091: Maid to Order	2001	8	$175-$250
Hum 2092: Make Me Pretty	2001	8	$175-$250
Hum 2093: Pretzel Boy	1999	8	$150-$190
Hum 2094: Christmas Wish	1999	7-8	$50-$175
Hum 2095: Proclamation	2006	8	$150-$200
Hum 2096/A through 2096/V: Angel Symphony series	1999, 2000	7-8	$95-$135 ea.
Hum 2097: Can I Play?	2006	8	$930-$1,250
Hum 2098: Annual Ornament Series	Various	8	$10-$20 ea.
Hum 2099/A: Saint Nicholas Day ornament	2000	8	$10-$20
Hum 2100: Picture Perfect	2000	8	$2,800-$3,495
Hum 2101/A: A Girl's Best Friend	2001	8	$75-$135
Hum 2101/B: A Boy's Best Friend	2001	8	$75-$135

Hum 2079/B: Windy Wishes

Hum 2082: Oh, No!

Hum 2084/A: Jump for Joy

Hum 2084/B: Count Me In

Hum 2085: Little Farm Hand

Hum 2086: Spring Sowing

Hum 2087/A: Sharpest Student

Hum 2087/B: Honor Student

Hum 2088/A: Playing Around

Hum 2088/B: Rolling Around

Hum 2089/A: Looking Around

Hum 2089/B: Waiting Around

Hum 2091: Maid to Order

Hum 2092: Make Me Pretty

Hum 2093: Pretzel Boy

Hum 2094: Christmas Wish

Hum 2095: Proclamation

Hum 2100: Picture Perfect

Hum No./Name	Year	Trademarks	Value
Hum 2102/A: My Heart's Desire	2002	8	$105-$140
Hum 2102/B: Secret Admirer	2002	8	$105-$140
Hum 2103/A: Puppet Princess	2001	8	$55-$90
Hum 2103/B: Puppet Prince	2001	8	$55-$90
Hum 2104: Sunflower Friends	2001	8	$195
Hum 2105: Miss Behaving	2001	8	$240
Hum 2106: Christmas Time	2001	8	$40-$200
Hum 2107/A: Bee Hopeful	2000	8	$150-$175
Hum 2107/B: Little Knitter	2001	8	$150-$175
Hum 2108/A: Musik Please	2002	8	$150-$175

Hum 2101/A: A Girl's Best Friend

Hum 2101/B: A Boy's Best Friend

Hum 2102/A: My Heart's Desire

Hum 2102/B: Secret Admirer

Hum 2103/A:
Puppet Princess

Hum 2103/B:
Puppet Prince

Hum 2104:
Sunflower Friends

Hum 2105: Miss Beehaving

Hum 2106: Christmas Time   Hum 2107/A: Bee Hopeful

Hum No./Name	Year	Trademarks	Value
Hum 2108/B: Alpine Dancer	2001	8	$150-$175
Hum 2109: Open Number			
Hum 2110/A: Christmas Delivery ornament	1999	7-8	$10-$20
Hum 2111/A: Making New Friends ornament	1999	7-8	$10-$20
Hum 2112: Open Number			
Hum 2113: Extra! Extra!	2001	8	$175-$250
Hum 2114: Declaration of Freedom	2004	8	$250-$350
Hum 2115: Lantern Fun	2004	8	$75-$99
Hum 2116/A: One Cup of Sugar	2001	8	$75-$125
Hum 2116/B: Baking Time	2001	8	$75-$125
Hum 2117-2119: Open Numbers			
Hum 2120: Little Miss Mail Carrier	2004	8	$200-$250
Hum 2121: Soap Box Derby	2002	8	$900-$1,250

Hum 2107/B: Little Knitter

Hum 2108/A: Musik Please

Hum 2108/B: Alpine Dancer

Hum 2113: Extra! Extra!

Hum 2114:
Declaration of Freedom

Hum 2115: Lantern Fun

Hum 2116/A: One Cup of Sugar

Hum 2116/B: Baking Time

Hummel® Listings

Hum No./Name	Year	Trademarks	Value
Hum 2122: Sweet Nap	2009	9	$299
Hum 2123: Open Number			
Hum 2124: Summer Adventure	2002	8	$475-$695
Hum 2125: Teacher's Pet	2002	8	$110-$175
Hum 2126-2128: Open Numbers			
Hum 2129/A: Ring in the Season ornament	2002	8	$10-$20
Hum 2130: Nutcracker Sweet	2002	8	$150-$250
Hum 2131: Open Number			
Hum 2132: Camera Ready	2002	8	$265-$475
Hum 2133: Bashful Serenade	2002	8	$400-$475
Hum 2134: Wintertime Duet	2002	8	$150-$175
Hum 2135/A: Angelic Drummer	2005	8	$100-$139
Hum 2135/C: Precious Pianist	2005	8	$165-$219
Hum 2135/D: Melodic Mandolin	2003	8	$100-$139
Hum 2135/E: Celestial Dreamer	2003	8	$100-$139
Hum 2135/F: Sounds of Joy	2003	8	$145-$179
Hum 2135/G: Rejoice	2002	8	$100-$145
Hum 2135/H: Angelic Trumpeter	2003	8	$100-$145
Hum 2135/J: Spirited Saxophonist	2004	8	$100-$165
Hum 2135/K: Angel With Triangle	2005	8	$100-$165
Hum 2135/L: Angel With Carillon	2007	8	$100-$165
Hum 2135/M: Angel With Accordion	2008	8	$100-$165
Hum 2136: The Cat's Meow	2003	8	$175-$300
Hum 2137-2142: Open Numbers			
Hum 2143/A: Season's Best	2002	8	$165-$220
Hum 2143/B: Let's Take to the Ice	2002	8	$165-$220
Hum 2144-2147: Open Numbers			
Hum 2148/A: Wait for Me	2002	8	$50-$100
Hum 2148/B: First Mate	2002	8	$50-$100
Hum 2149: Open Number			

Hum 2120:
Little Miss Mail Carrier

Hum 2122: Sweet Nap

Hum 2124: Summer Adventure

Hum 2125: Teacher's Pet

Hum 2130: Nutcracker Sweet

Hum 2132:
Camera Ready

Hum 2133: Bashful Serenade

Hum 2134: Wintertime Duet

Hum 2135/A: Angelic Drummer

Hum 2135/C: Precious Pianist

Hum 2135/D: Melodic Mandolin

Hum 2135/E: Celestial Dreamer

Hum 2135/F: Sounds of Joy

Hum No./Name	Year	Trademarks	Value
Hum 2150/A: Perfect Pitch	2007	8	$279
Hum 2150/B: Cheerful Tune	2007	8	$329
Hum 2151: Open Number			
Hum 2152/A: Dearly Beloved trinket box	2003	8	$50
Hum 2153: Big Announcement	2003	8	$80-$165
Hum 2154/A: Patriotic Spirit	2002	8	$150-$198

Hum 2135/H: Angelic Trumpeter

Hum 2135/G: Rejoice

Hum 2135/J: Spirited Saxophonist

Hum 2135/K: Angel With Triangle

Hum 2135/L: Angel With Carillon

Hum 2135/M:
Angel With Accordion

Hum 2136: The Cat's Meow

Hum 2143/A: Season's Best

Hum 2148/A: Wait For Me

Hum 2148/B: First Mate

Hum 2150/A: Perfect Pitch

Hum 2153: Big Announcement

Hum 2155: Teddy Tales

Hum 2156: Loads of Fun

Hum No./Name	Year	Trademarks	Value
Hum 2154/B: Celebration of Freedom	2002	8	$150-$198
Hum 2155: Teddy Tales	2006	8	$154-$199
Hum 2156: Loads of Fun	2007	8	$249
Hum 2157: Full Speed Ahead/ When I Grow Up	2003	8	$150-$300
Hum 2158-2161: Open Numbers			
Hum 2162: Baker's Delight	2004	8	$950-$1,200
Hum 2163/A: Dearly Beloved ornament	2003	8	$25
Hum 2164: Me and My Shadow (with Steiff bear)	2002	8	$350-$450
Hum 2165: Farm Days	2003	8	$1,000-$1,200
Hum 2166: Circus Act	2003	8	$199

Steiff bear and Hum 2164: Me and My Shadow set

Hum No./Name	Year	Trademarks	Value
Hum 2167: Mixing the Cake	2004	8	$200-$300
Hum 2168: Today's Recipe	2004	8	$200-$300
Hum 2169-2170: Open Numbers			
Hum 2171/A: Pretty Performer	2003	8	$185
Hum 2171/B: Serenade of Songs	2003	8	$185
Hum 2172: Open Number			
Hum 2173: First Flight	2003	8	$150-$200
Hum 2174/A: Pretty Posey	2004	8	$80-$110
Hum 2174/B: Pocket Full of Posies	2004	8	$80-$110
Hum 2175: From the Pumpkin Patch	2006	8	$120-$150
Hum 2176: Open Number			
Hum 2177: Shall We Dance	2003	8	$185-$325

Hum 2165: Farm Days

Hum 2171/A: Pretty Performer   Hum 2171/B: Serenade of Songs

Hum 2173: First Flight

Hum 2175:
From the Pumpkin Patch

Hum No./Name	Year	Trademarks	Value
Hum 2178/A and 2179/A: Bridal Gifts	2003	8	$50-$75
Hum 2180: The Final Sculpt	2002	8	$250-$499
Hum 2181: Clear as a Bell	2004	8	$100
Hum 2182: First Solo	2003	8	$100
Hum 2183: Keeping Time	2006	8	$100
Hum 2184: First Violin	2005	8	$100
Hum 2185: Winter's Here	2003	8	$250
Hum 2186: Open Number			
Hum 2187: Benevolent Birdfeeder	2003	8	$439
Hum 2188-2189: Open Numbers			
Hum 2190: Harvest Time	2003	8	$3,500
Hum 2191-2192: Open Numbers			
Hum 2193/4/0: Flowers for Mother	2004	8	$100

Hum 2181: Clear as a Bell

Hum 2182: First Solo

Hum 2183: Keeping Time

Hum 2184: First Violin

Hum 2185: Winter's Here

Hum 2187: Benevolent Birdfeeder

Hum 2190: Harvest Time

Hum 2193/4/0: Flowers for Mother   Hum 2195: Sunflower Girl

Hum No./Name	Year	Trademarks	Value
Hum 2194: Duty Calls	2003	8	$250-$400
Hum 2195/4/0: Sunflower Girl	2004	8	$100
Hum 2196: Open Number			
Hum 2197: American Spirit	2003	8	$250
Hum 2198: Melody Conductor	2006	8	$100
Hum 2199: Baby Steps	2007	8	$329
Hum 2200: Autumn Time	2005	8	$2,000-$3,000
Hum 2201: Baby's First Drawing	2008	8	$299
Hum 2202: Open Number			
Hum 2203: Hope	2004	8	$99
Hum 2204: Holiday Fun	2004	8	$230
Hum 2205: Troublemaker	2005	8	$1,200

Hum 2197: American Spirit

Hum 2198: Melody Conductor

Hum 2200: Autumn Time

Hum 2203: Hope

Hum 2204: Holiday Fun

Hum 2205: Troublemaker

Hum No./Name	Year	Trademarks	Value
Hum 2206-2208: Open Numbers			
Hum 2209/A: Puppet Love	2004	8	$139
Hum 2209/B: Puppet Pal	2004	8	$139
Hum 2210: Open Number			
Hum 2211: Fancy Footwork	2005	8	$179
Hum 2212: Keeper of the Goal	N/A	8	$179
Hum 2213: Open Number			
Hum 2214: What a Smile	2005	8	$279
Hum 2215: Gotcha!	2005	8	$279
Hum 2216: Homecoming	2005	8	$300-$450
Hum 2217/A: Do You Love It!	2005	8	$99
Hum 2217/B: Look What I Made	2005	8	$99
Hum 2218: Springtime Friends	2005	8	$99
Hum 2219: Sunflower Boy	2005	8	$99
Hum 2220: School Days	2005	8	$99
Hum 2221: All Bundled Up	2005	8	$99
Hum 2222: A Star for You	2005	8	$359
Hum 2223: Practice Makes Perfect (girl)	2005	8	$139
Hum 2224-2225: Open Numbers			
Hum 2226: Shepherd's Apprentice	2005	8	$139
Hum 2227: Morning Call	2005	8	$139
Hum 2228: Can't Catch Me	2005	8	$129
Hum 2229: Puppy Pal	2005	8	$99
Children's Nativity Sets			
Hum 2230/A: Mary	2005	8	$149
Hum 2230/B: Joseph	2005	8	$149
Hum 2230/C: Child Jesus With Manger	2005	8	$149
Hum 2230/D: Shepherd With Staff	2005	8	$149
Hum 2230/E: Shepherd With Milk Jug	2005	8	$149

Hum 2209/A: Puppet Love   Hum 2209/B: Puppet Pal

Hum 2211: Fancy Footwork   Hum 2212: Keeper of the Goal

Hum 2214: What a Smile

Hum 2215: Gotcha!

Hum 2217/A: Do You Love It!

Hum 2217/B: Look What I Made!

Hum 2228: Can't Catch Me

Hum 2229: Puppy Pal

Hum 2231: Friendly Feeding

Hum 2232: Let's Be Friends

Hum 2233:
Light of Hope

Hum 2234:
Night Before Christmas

Hum No./Name	Year	Trademarks	Value
Hum 2230/F: Shepherd With Flute	2005	8	$149
Hum 2230/G: King Melchior	2005	8	$149
Hum 2230/H: King Balthazar	2005	8	$149
Hum 2230/J: King Gaspar	2005	8	$149
Hum 2230/K: Angel With Lantern	2005	8	$149
Hum 2230/L: Angela	2005	8	$99
Hum 2230/M: Young Calf	2005	8	$35
Hum 2230/N: Donkey	2005	8	$35
Hum 2230/O: Sheep, Laying	2005	8	$20
Hum 2230/P: Sheep, Standing	2005	8	$25
Hum 2230/S: Watchful Vigil	2007	8	$149
Hum 2230/T: Little Blessings	2007	8	$99
Hum 2231: Friendly Feeding	2005	8	$139
Hum 2232: Let's Be Friends	2005	8	$125
Hum 2233: Light of Hope	2005	8	$99

Hum 2235: Lucky Friend   Hum 2236: Sleigh Ride

Hum No./Name	Year	Trademarks	Value
Hum 2234: Night Before Christmas	2005	8	$230
Hum 2235: Lucky Friend	2006	8	$219
Hum 2236: Sleigh Ride	2005	8	$139
Hum 2237: Sunday Stroll	2006	8	$199
Hum 2238-2239: Open Numbers			
Hum 2240: Heart of Hope	2006	8	$100
Hum 2241: Coming from the Woods	2006	8	$219-$259
Hum 2242: Spring Step	N/A	8	$125
Hum 2243: Spring Tune	N/A	8	$125
Hum 2244: Spring Song	N/A	8	$125
Hum 2245: Spring Sweetheart	N/A	8	$125
Hum 2246: Let Me Help You	2007	8	$299
Hum 2247: Gretl	2007	8	$219
Hum 2248: Special Delivery	2006	8	$350

Hum 2237: Sunday Stroll

Hum 2240: Heart of Hope

Hum 2241: Coming From the Woods

Hum 2242: Spring Step

Hum 2243: Spring Tune

Hum 2244: Spring Song

Hum 2245: Spring Sweetheart

Hum 2246: Let Me Help You

Hum 2247: Gretl   Hum 2248: Special Delivery

Hum No./Name	Year	Trademarks	Value
Hum 2249: Marmalade Lover	2008	8	$289
Hum 2250: Learning to Share	2006	8	$1,200
Hum 2251: Swimming Lesson	2007	8	$99
Hum 2252: Joys of Hope	2007	8	$219
Hum 2253: Open Number			
Hum 2254: Susi	2008	8	$159
Hum 2255: Forever Friends	2007	8	$2,750
Hum 2256: Open Number			
Hum 2257: Little Concerto	N/A	8	$219
Hum 2258: For Mommy	N/A	8	$219
Hum 2259: A Gift For You	2008	8	$179
Hum 2260: Open Number			
Hum 2261: Story Time	2008	8	$1,000
Hum 2262: How Can I Help You?	2007	8	$169

Hum 2250: Learning to Share

Hum 2251:
Swimming Lesson

Hum 2252: Joy of Hope
with pink ribbon base

Hum 2254: Susi

Hum 2255: Forever Friends

Hum No./Name	Year	Trademarks	Value
Hum 2263: Christmas Morning	2006	8	$600
Hum 2264: Christmas Treat	2007	8	$219
Hum 2265: She Caught It	2008	8	$349
Hum 2266: Mayor	2008	8	$99
Hum 2267: Little Cobbler	2007	8	$99
Hum 2268: Littlest Teacher	2008	8	$99
Hum 2269: Be My Guest	2008	8	$99
Hum 2270: Little Seamstress	2008	8	$99
Hum 2271: Proud Baker	2008	8	$99
Hum 2272: Market Girl	2008	8	$99
Hum 2273: Spring Gifts	N/A	8	$125
Hum 2274: Ready to Play	2007	8	$179
Hum 2275: Summer Castles	2008	8	$269
Hum 2276: Summer Delight	2008	8	$269

Hum 2263/A & B: Christmas Morning   Hum 2264: Christmas Treat

Hum No./Name	Year	Trademarks	Value
Hum 2277/A: Follow Your Heart	N/A	8	$119
Hum 2277/B: With All My Heart	N/A	8	$119
Hum 2278: Just Ducky	2008	8	$50
Hum 2279: Look At Me!	N/A	8	$229
Hum 2280: Christmas Duet Collector's Set	2008	8	$229
Hum 2281: Puppy's Bath	2009	9	$379
Hum 2282/A: Precious Bouquet	2009	9	$219
Hum 2282/B: Full of Charm	2009	9	$219
Hum 2283/II: Winter Friend	2008	8	$500
Hum 2284: Butterfly Wishes	2008	8	$350
Hum 2285: Strolling With Friends	2009	9	$529
Hum 2287: Wishing on a Star	2010	9	$169
Hum 2288: Sister's Children	2009	9	$6,750

Hum 2265: She Caught It!   Hum 2266: Mayor

Hum No./Name	Year	Trademarks	Value
Hum 2290: Sailing Lesson	2009	9	$1,700
Hum 2291/A: Up and Down	2011	9	$349
Hum 2292-2293: Open Numbers			
Hum 2294: Hope for Tomorrow	2010	9	$169
Hum 2295: Open Number			
Hum 2296: Little Luck	2010	9	$55
Hum 2297: A Lucky Bug	N/A	9	$55
Hum 2297: A Lucky Bug key ring	N/A	9	$10
Hum 2298-2300: Open Numbers			
Hum 2301: Sparkling Shell	2010	9	$459
Hum 2302: Open Number			
Hum 2303: Giddy Up	2010	9	$299
Hum 2304-2308: Open Numbers			
Hum 2309/A: Just for You	2010	9	$359

Hum No./Name	Year	Trademarks	Value
Hum 2309/B: Only for You	2010	9	$359
Hum 2310: Precious Pony	2010	9	$229
Hum 2311: Curious Colt	2010	9	$229
Hum 2312: Teeter-Totter Time	2010	9	$1,100
Hum 2313: No Bed Please	2010	9	$189
Hum 2314: First Piano Lesson	2010	9	$299
Hum 2315/N: 2009 Annual Angel	2009	N/A	$99
Hum 2318/A: A Prayer for You	2011	9	$179
Hum 2318/B: A Prayer for Everyone	2011	9	$179
Hum 2320: Follow That Fawn	2011	9	$3,200
Hum 2322/A: Baby Boy (Alfred)	2011	9	$179
Hum 2322/B: Baby Girl (Traundl)	2011	9	$179
Hum 2323: Sweetheart	2011	9	N/A
Hum 2324: Cuddly Calf	2011	9	$249
Hum 2325: Prized Pig	2011	9	$229
Hum 2326: Hee Haw	2011	9	$299
Hum 2327: Angel of Hope annual angel	2011	9	$179
Hum 2328: Shine So Bright	2011	9	$619
Hum 2329: A Simple Wish	2011	9	$179
Hum 2330: Song of Hope	2011	9	$179
Hum 2333: Tag Along Teddy	2011	9	$1,800
Hum 2358: Noisemakers	2011	9	$1,400
Hum 3012, 3015-3021: Ball Ornaments	N/A	8	$30-$40 ea.

Index

2009 Annual Angel: Hum 2315/N 498
Accompanist, The: Hum 453 . . . . 299, 301
Accordion Ballad: Hum 857 408
Accordion Boy: Hum 185 . . . . 182, 184
Adieu plaque: Hum 820 406
Adoration bookends: Hum 90/B 141, 143
Adoration With Bird: Hum 105 146-147
Adoration: Hum 23 93-94
    Adoring Children: Hum 903 . . . . . 418, 420
Advent Group: Hum 31 103
Adventure Bound: Hum 347 . . . . 229, 243
African Wanderer: Hum 2062 441
Afternoon Nap annual plate: Hum 922 422
Afternoon Nap: Hum 836 . . . . 406, 411
All Aboard1997: Hum 2044 . . . . 438, 443
All Bundled Up: Hum 2221 . . . . 485, 488
All By Myself: Hum 2079/A 446, 453
All Smiles: Hum 498 . . . . 307, 326
Alpine Dancer: Hum 2108/B 463-464
American Spirit: Hum 2197 482-483
American Wanderer: Hum 2061 441
Angel at Prayer holy water font:
    Hum 91/A and 91/B. 141, 144
Angel Cloud holy water font: Hum 206 193
Angel Duet candleholder: Hum 193 . . . 186-187
Angel Duet holy water font: Hum 146 . . 163-164
Angel Duet: Hum 261 211-212
Angel Joyous News With Trumpet holy water font:
    Hum 242. . . . . 202, 206
Angel Lights candleholder: Hum 241 . .202, 206
Angel of Hope: Hum 2327 498
Angel Serenade With Lamb: Hum 83 . . 138-139
Angel Shrine holy water font: Hum 147 . 163-164
Angel Symphony series: Hum 2096/A
    through 2096/V. 454
Angel Trio: Hum 38, 39, and 40 110-112
Angel With Accordion: Hum 2135/M . . . 466, 473
Angel With Bird holy water font: Hum 167 . .168, 171
Angel With Bird holy water font: Hum 22 92
Angel With Carillon: Hum 2135/L 466, 473
Angel With Lantern, Angel With Trumpet, and
    Angel With Bird holy water fonts:

Hum 354/A-C 244, 247
Angel With Lantern: Hum 2230/K 489
Angel With Lute, Angel With Accordion, Angel
    With Trumpet angel trio set: Hum 238/A-C
    199-200
Angel With Triangle: Hum 2135/K . . . 466, 472
Angel With Two Children at Feet plaque:
    Hum 108. . . . . 146, 148
Angela: Hum 2230/L 489
Angelic Drummer: Hum 2135/A 466, 469
Angelic Guide Christmas ornament:
    Hum 571. . . . . 324, 339
Angelic Sleep candleholder: Hum 25 96
Angelic Song: Hum 144 162-163
Angelic Trumpeter: Hum 2135/H 466, 472
Angler, The: Hum 566. . . . . 324, 337
Anniversary Plates: Hum 280-282 216
Annual Ornament Series: Hum 2098 454
Annual Plates: Hum 264-279, 283-291 . . . 211
Apple a Day, An: Hum 403 . . . . 278, 277
Apple Tree Boy bookends: Hum 252/A . . 205-206
Apple Tree Boy doll: Hum 951 422
Apple Tree Boy table lamp: Hum 230 200
Apple Tree Boy: Hum 142 162
Apple Tree Girl and Apple Tree Boy
    candleholders: Hum 676, 677 365
Apple Tree Girl bookends: Hum 252/B . . 205-206
Apple Tree Girl doll: Hum 950 422
Apple Tree Girl table lamp: Hum 229 200
Apple Tree Girl: Hum 141 161-162
April Showers: Hum 610 . . . . 340, 348
Arithmetic Lesson: Hum 303 . . . . . 213, 216
Art Critic: Hum 318. . . . . 216, 222
Artist, The, display plaque: Hum 756 385
Artist, The: Hum 304 . . . . 213, 216
Asian Wanderer: Hum 2063 441
At Grandpa's: Hum 621. . . . . 346, 354
At Play: Hum 632 . . . . 347, 360
At the Fence: Hum 324 224-225
Auf Wiedersehen: Hum 153 . . . . 164, 167
Australian Wanderer: Hum 2064 441
Autumn Harvest: Hum 355 . . . . 244, 248

Index

Index

Index

Index

Index

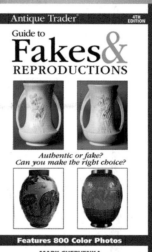